From Birth to Death
With Sex In Between

By

Marshu W. Caspe, M. E.

First Edition

ISBN 978-0-9995020-1-3

About the Author

Therapist Marshu W. Caspe is the founder of Life Motivating Counseling Inc. and the "Journey to Now Protocol". She holds a Student Personnel Counseling M. E. from the State of New Jersey and a Rape Crisis Counseling Certification from New York Planned Parenthood. She is a licensed New York State Mental Health Counselor. Ms. Caspe's therapy practice with Life Motivating Counseling Inc. has been ongoing for the past thirty-three years.

e-mail
contact@marshuwcaspe.com

Dedication

I dedicate this book to my husband, Manny, for his patience and caring to co-edit countless times since 2008. My son, Lee and his wife Kathy took the time from their complicated lives to show their love and devotion by editing the final manuscript. Lee is the cover artist. The four of us grew closer on deeper levels from sharing this work. Manny, Lee and Kathy's verbal challenges were an important part of my growth process.

Acknowledgement

THANK YOU for all your encouraging words. In 2013, my rolfer Steven Glassman was the first to read the original eighty-five pages of *From Birth to Death with Sex In Between*. He said, "It's good" and that gave me hope. My friend Carol Haber, a retired newspaper editor, read that same manuscript and said, "I love it." That inspired me. Dr. Gary Null is an internationally known advocate for informed health and political choice. He read that same manuscript and said, "It's good" and I was delighted. My soul sister Dina Grinshpun always expressed her excitement for my work. My daughter Lyn encouraged me. My husband Manny always praised my creative efforts. He supported me from my first attempt to put the protocol into words that were understandable and beneficial for the reader. Finally, my friend Maritza Garcia, a legal assistant, proofread the book with critical love.

It was when Maritza asked me to please tell her what my book was about, that I kiddingly said, *From Birth to Death with Sex In Between*. Maritza said, "I'm going to buy THAT book" and I knew this was going to be the title I would use.

Inttoduction

ARE YOU…

- Choosing stressful relationships?

- Fearing change?

- Coping with the loss of a loved one?

- Reliving childhood traumas?

- Struggling with chemical or emotional addiction?

YOU CAN…
Free yourself of conflict, anxiety and stress quickly with FROM
BIRTH TO DEATH WITH SEX IN BETWEEN

Trauma, uncertainty and struggle can be transformed into a life of clarity, assurance and joy with Marshu Caspe's engaging personal memoir. Included is a complete self-help guide, the *Journey to Now Protocol*, a resource for conquering self-doubt and fear. Discover who you really are and live it NOW.

Table of Contents

CHAPTER 1

Kerhonkson 1937, From a Secret Place
in the Woods to Karma

Thick green moss was our Persian carpet. A circle of tall pines guarded our secret hiding place deep in the woods. Our path wound from a creek through a forested area and across railroad tracks, leading to more trees and a large expanse of flat rock. There we let the sun warm us while we feasted on berries we picked. The crows cawed, we mimicked them, and they answered. We explored surrounding wooded areas where we could gently touch and smell the beautiful wildflowers, searching for different kinds of butterflies.

Our journey to the creek was a daily ritual for the women and girls. Once there, without any embarrassment, we took off our bathing suits and carried soap and washcloths into the water. The women caringly soaped each other's backs and long hair. They would join hands in a circle, jump up and down together and laugh with joyful "ahhs!" Their enormous breasts also jumped up and down and when at rest they formed a circular flotilla of mammary glands bobbing on the surface of the water. My friend Shirley and I giggled with the women whose unadulterated playful pleasure created a beautiful, earthy vision.

These women were totally unaware of the wonderful picture they created, washing each other and swimming with no modesty or self-consciousness. The body was just accepted as a part of the person. At the end of this ritual we climbed out of the water, towel dried ourselves and put on our bathing suits for the walk back to our "resort." The men had their own bathing time, but it was fun when everyone joined together, playfully wrestling, splashing and dunking. Amid that deeply wooded area, at this isolated part of the creek we relished the women's gleeful reactions to "surprise" water attacks.

Air currents urge the graceful tree branches to bend.
Dainty leaves create a unity of movement.
Lush full leafy green costumes that are protruding
Escort our car just like two chorus lines dancing...

My eleven-year-old imagination played with that vision of the tree-lined roads. They guided our first four-hour journey to Kerhonkson, New York in the summer of 1937. We took that trip for the next six years.

Kerhonkson was the first setting where I experienced an environment that harmonized with my inner tranquility. Eventually that compatibility allowed me to realize the possibility of learning to live in the NOW.

Joe, the owner of a Kerhonkson "resort," grew up in the same Ukrainian community as my parents, which meant they were "Landsmen." How Joe managed to get a mortgage on his meager income we could never understand. He called on his Landsmen to help him survive. Everyone came to his rescue by spending happy summers at his "resort." He was a tailor and a philosopher who fancied himself to be a "fixer-upper." We loved him and giggled at the results of his imperfect labor. In one apartment, we discovered a closet with a bathtub and no water connections. On one occasion that turned out be helpful. One of the women decided to be "ultra-natural" and rather than rush back to the house, she relieved herself in the woods. She had no toilet paper so she wiped her rear end with any available leaves. Unbeknownst to her, this was poison ivy. Not surprisingly, she suffered agonizing itching in some very sensitive places. The other women quickly came to her rescue and created a relief-line of pots with hot water and Epsom salts to fill that tub in the closet. It helped soothe that poor woman's misery.

At this establishment, there was a wooden main building painted white, much like the other houses on that road. There was another small,

4

unpainted bungalow with three separate and very compact family units. The wall between my parents' unit and our Landsman Gussie was a pine board with a knot hole, through which Gussie and I laughingly passed matches and other essentials of life. There were two bathrooms in the main house, one directly above the other, with the cracked ceiling of the downstairs bathroom being the cracked floor of the upper one. My friend Shirley and I thought it was fun to occupy both bathrooms at the same time and pass notes and have conversations through the cracks. Our luxurious outdoor shower was in a shed that opened to the sky. Everybody shared the shower with a procession of daddy long legs spiders. This was acceptable because we mostly bathed in the creek.

The dining area was in an unfinished, bare wood extension to the main house. It had a very large room in which each family had their designated table placed against the outer walls. In an adjoining room, they had their own refrigerators, stoves but only one oven was available. There, lively conversations and recipes were shared.

The "landsmen" families spent summers together at the resort. The elders created a feeling of camaraderie by sharing their childhood experiences and comparing their adventurous journeys from Russia to America. Comedic pranksters told jokes and funny stories about their Russian childhoods, of people they knew and current issues. There were outdoor parties with large glasses of hot tea sweetened with fruits and jams. Each weekend we shared cakes and cookies the women baked to celebrate their husbands' return. We relaxed lying on the grass or on spread-out blankets. Sometimes, Shirley and I would lie flat on the grass at night, looking up at the sky. The moving clouds made us feel as though we were floating off the earth, so we locked hands for safety. The elders enjoyed the sunshine and pure mountain air, breathing in deeply and exhaling loudly with pure pleasure. The children watched, embraced those feelings of communal harmony and felt that they were an integral part of the social activities. With no television, the evening entertainment for children included listening to the adults' stories, singing old Russian folk songs and taking long after-dinner walks along country roads. The children used jars to make "lightning bug flashlights" to guide their evening walks. It didn't work, and the lightning bugs were mercifully given their freedom.

Music was an important part of socializing amongst these families that came from pre-Stalin Russia and we sang their Russian folk songs together. It was our good fortune that a Kerhonkson neighbor was disposing of her grandmother's beautiful old pump organ. We rescued it and brought it into our dining hall to polish and tune it. One family taught us how to love and respect music even more than we did. Their daughter Sylvia, a piano teacher, played the organ for us.

On a Friday night, the husbands' first night back from the city, the older adults were sure to get to bed early. The younger adults decided to carry the organ through the woods to "the rocks." Without any elders to watch, we took a small token of an egg, a bit of salami or a slice of onion from each refrigerator for our bonfire and made a delicious midnight snack. Sylvia played Bach in the woods. Shirley and I, lying on a blanket, closed our eyes and breathed in the music. During the day, we explored an unkempt root cellar which was a storage place for unwanted stuff. We found a wind-up Victrola, and Enrique Caruso records. We played Caruso's sublime recording of The Pearl Fishers in the root cellar. I can still hear it and I still love it.

Many decades later I spoke to Shirley about this book and Kerhonkson. I thought that it was just me who thought those summer experiences were the happiest time of my childhood, but Shirley felt the same way. She wisely said that the joy we experienced was probably true for the adults as well in that pre-World War II era. It was so moving to know how much we both remembered details of the joy we shared.

Shirley was the daughter of the "resort" owners. We laughingly called this resort the "Sunshine Villa." Shirley and I laughed a lot together. We had our meals together. She shared my bed because all the other units were rented. That income was essential for her family's survival. These nights gave us more time to think up adventures. At eleven we were as sophisticated as three-year-olds are today and we planned our future. I wanted to be a ballet dancer and Shirley wanted to become a dress designer.

Continuous rain for three days found Shirley and I shut in, getting bored and restless. We decided that we wanted to eat corn and a neighboring farm had an extensive acreage of corn. We didn't think the farmer would mind if we "borrowed" six ears of corn. We set out on our mission. The ground was muddy and we kept our bodies low so as not to be seen. With six ears of corn in our possession we were ready to retreat. A sudden sound of gunfire shocked and frightened us. We fell flat into the deep mud and running for cover I lost a shoe. Back at "Sunshine Villa," we were ready to cook our corn, but Shirley's mother said, "That's not people corn, it's cow corn!" We were disappointed for a split second and then bent over with laughter.

Some evenings, Shirley and I put on our "good clothes" and walked the four miles on dark roads to "town." It was only one block long, with some utility stores, including a post office and a deli with a jukebox. Across the main highway was an inn. It had a restaurant and a bar which was a social gathering place. Everyone from the judge, to the doctor, to the town drunk, congregated there without a social caste system.

Shirley and I went into town looking for boys, yet we generally wound up just socializing with all the townspeople. There were no "summer people" in this town at night because there were no attractions for them. But the important thing for me was that I was accepted by the Kerhonksonians. At first, I was just summer people, but I began to be accepted as one of the town people because I was always with my Kerhonksonian friend.

Serenity

There is nothing so serene
As dignity of trees
Stretching their foliage
Towards the bright sun's image

Nesting in that slow dance
Growing from, giving to
Its birth center anew.

This was a period prior to World War II when we felt safe in our environment. Shirley and I stayed in the woods or sat in the creek all day. We watched the tiny minnows swimming around our legs through that clean, clear water. We only came home for food and no one asked us how, why, or where we had been. Our parents knew we were safe and we were. In Kerhonkson, I found a serene and happy environment outside of myself. I belonged, and I felt secure. I loved the kind of socialization you can find in a small community, especially when I was accepted as part of it.

At summer's end, I cried, and I begged to be left behind in Kerhonkson to live with Shirley and her family. My parents ignored me. Traveling home on the George Washington Bridge, I saw the grey New York City skyline and I was broken-hearted. I asked if I could just be allowed to WALK back to Kerhonkson. I wonder if anyone in my family understood my grief because no one said anything to acknowledge it.

Kerhonkson, for many years into adulthood, was my gut home. I returned at various times. Once I went back when I needed the serenity to decipher a traumatic moment in my life. At that time, it was the only place where I could breathe peacefully and reevaluate my life's journey. I went back to reconnect. And I went back to Kerhonkson for romance.

Kerhonkson was my realization that I could harmonize my inner being with my environment and feel safe and tranquil. Since my first journey to Kerhonkson at the age of eleven on into adulthood, I had experienced love, joy, anger, tragedy and accomplishments in my life. It wasn't until I became a **Nichiren Shoshu Buddhist** in 1974 that I fully understood the possibility of transforming life's unhappy circumstances, to really live the joyous and serene life that was within me. I realized how much the quality of my inner being affected my social environment. Studying the Buddhist concept of karma. I understood it as a repetitive energy functioning pattern. This led to the concept of trauma recycling and the development of the ***Journey to Now Protocol***. This program illustrates how emotional and physical pain caused by traumatic experiences can be transformed into joyful ones. I learned the Nichiren Shoshu Buddhist concept that one can only change one's own karma and not someone else's. This influenced the development of **Life Motivating Counseling**, a short-term reality based therapy. It focuses on one's responsibility for adjusting immediate social interactions. The *Journey to Now* and **Understanding Addiction** evolved and became extensions of *Life Motivating Counseling*.

From a secret place in the woods, to karma, to the *Journey to Now*, I am enjoying the ongoing adventure living the reality of NOW. I offer you this guide towards your destination.

It was our first summer weekend in Kerhonkson. My father liked having his family around him, enjoying each other's company. Sam led the activities. He brought a badminton set and appointed me caretaker when he wasn't there. Clockwise: brother Ruby, father Jack, sister Sally, mother Sonetta (legally blind), brother Sam, me.

Shirley is lying on the grass at the "Sunshine Villa." In the background, Sonya is resting in a beach chair. I didn't know she had cancer and this was to be her last summer. Sonya's sister Gussie stayed very close to her all that season.

Tea time at "Sunshine Villa". Clockwise: Joe, his wife Gussie, Bea, cousin Dora, Shirley, Bea's husband, Gussie, Zonevela and his wife Sonya pouring hot tea into large glasses.

CHAPTER 2

The Path Evolved

I was the "baby" of four siblings and my formative years were spent primarily with caretaking adults. I was always in need of my mother's constant care due to illness and surgeries. Doctors made home visits to their patients at that time. A doctor who had to visit me frequently came to treat my grippe. Standing in front of me, he gave his diagnosis to my mother. "If we put her in a glass cage, maybe she'll grow up." Sorry to contradict that doctor, but I'm still alive at age ninety.

A six-year difference between me and my sister separated us socially. A ten and twelve-year difference between me and my two older brothers created more of a social disconnect. I was the baby of the family and had an affectionate relationship with my father, an older brother and cousins. They thought I was cute and they enjoyed my response to their loving attention. Some relatives thought I was a child with special qualities that weren't nurtured but their comments fell on deaf ears. As I grew older, my mother didn't consider my serious educational requests which could have helped me avoid a future of confusion and pain.

Saturdays were the special days my mother set aside for visiting relatives. My father worked until noon on Saturdays and then joined me and my mother wherever we were visiting. I was the family "baby" who accompanied my mother on these visits, while my older siblings were pursuing their own social interests.

I enjoyed the relaxed camaraderie of these social get-togethers. I heard the stories about past and present life experiences. The humorous tales they shared about themselves and others provoked easy laughter. I was especially close to one family, whose daughter, Sylvia would play the piano while we all sang. I felt a warm inner joy when I was with them. They showed a mutual respect and they could have fun together. It fulfilled my dream of being part of what an ideal family should be. In later years, Shirley and I reminisced about the first time we realized this kind of family could exist. The father, Zanevella, taught us Russian folk songs during our long summer evening walks in Kerhonkson. Through the years, he made me feel important, even though I was just a "kid."

The mother, Sonya, developed stomach cancer. I didn't know that it had progressed to the terminal stage. My mother woke me early one Saturday morning to tell me that she was visiting Sonya and she expected me to accompany her. I refused, and pretended that I was too sleepy to go. My mother went to visit Sonya by herself. It was her last visit with Sonya, who died soon after.

I felt guilty for not going to see Sonya for the last time. I wanted to show her that I loved her and I didn't do that. I felt as though I had abandoned Sonya at a time when she would have cherished that love. It was not until I was an adult, that I understood why I refused to visit her. I realized that I visualized and sensed other people's painful physical phenomenon. But as a teenager, I didn't understand my reaction to "seeing" the inside of Sonya's stomach and feeling her pain. I didn't know how to recognize or comprehend my experience. It was difficult to cope with my feelings. I sensed the pain of those who were suffering serious physical illnesses, which was uncomfortable and confusing, so I tried to avoid being near them. Into adulthood, I thought I was being squeamish about contracting someone's disease and I felt guilty about what I assumed was my lack of compassion. Now, I know that I was trying to get away from the pain I felt when I visualized someone else's physical problems, and I was unable to reckon with it.

Some relatives from pre-Stalin Russia accepted that they were psychic to some degree, and joked about their experiences. I knew which relatives were on the phone before I spoke to them and things that I envisioned did happen at a future time. When they did occur, I realized that I had already sensed those events and I just accepted these incidents. In the late sixties, I read *Psychic Discoveries Behind the Iron Curtain* by Sheila Ostrander and Lynn Schroeder. That clarified my thinking. This book describes various psychic and/or energy experiments and discoveries that helped me to understand my own experiences and capacities more clearly. It freed me to use that capacity in a constructive way for myself and others. In time, I accepted my ability to visualize a client's pain without verbalizing my observations and influencing the client. This was confirmed during the sessions, when clients would describe what I had sensed. My capacity enabled me to offer a more focused support for clients' in their journey to understand and ameliorate their anguish.

During counseling sessions, it became evident that painful emotional and physical sensations experienced in the present, were distinctly like those experienced during childhood traumas. The pain, fear and anger of those abrasive childhood encounters effects our behavior in the NOW. The continuum of these reenacted behaviors are old trauma reactions which cause emotional disturbances and are accompanied by discomforting body sensations.

Ongoing emotional and physical trauma that was imposed upon us at an earlier time influences our future behavior patterns. We do not connect those patterns to the reality of the moment, or who we are and can be. This emotionally conflicted socialization causes a mix of guilt, fear, inadequacy and distress to an already unnerving situation. The experience when using *Journey to Now* guides us to a rapid comprehension of the origins of existing emotional and physical pain. This enables the client to recognize how old trauma is being transposed into present relationships. The protocol helps you adjust your social behavior by learning how to live with who you really are. You no longer have to recycle old agonizing abuse reactions, but can react to life with a clear assessment of the HERE and NOW.

The basic reason clients came to my *Life Motivating Counseling* sessions was due to current social behavior problems. At these times, I observed ongoing correlations between original childhood traumas and repetitious troubling behavior. It motivated the development of *Journey to Now*. This made it possible for clients to recognize the recycling of old traumas. The experiential insight is the key that enables the clients to unlock the troubled behavior door and adjust current social interactions to their satisfaction.

"Alice" was fearful of reliving an emotionally panic-ridden childhood she experienced with her parents. She developed behavioral patterns of aggressive emotional and physical threats towards her children. Alice didn't realize she was making them afraid of her. This prevented them from getting physically and emotionally close enough to hurt her. She did not direct her aggression toward her parents who abused her, but she was harming the children instead. They became angry in response to her behavior and hurt her emotionally. The *Journey to Now Protocol* helped Alice realize where her fears and anger had originated. She understood that her present aggressive behavior was a reaction to her childhood trepidations. Alice could free herself from the shackles of her anguished childhood. She was now able to interact on a new level with her parents, who mistreated her in the past and indicated the kind of behavior she would accept in the present. She could clearly see current situations for what they are with her own family and she no longer reacted to the old traumas which had no relevance to the present. Alice developed an emotionally compassionate interaction with her children and parents and was definitely the victor. There was a scheduled meeting with her ex-husband. He became confused when he realized he was expected to react to her new behavior differently than he had in the past. Alice remained emotionally confident with the "terms" for social attitudes that she would accept or reject. Her ex-husband chose to respond to her new level of behavior in a pleasant manner, rather than be rejected by her. It proved to her that she felt secure with who she really was. Alice was no longer reliving the suffering she experienced in her childhood. She was very moved by her new freedom from fear and anger.

Hans Selye, in The *Stress of Life*, writes about the stresses and strains of everyday existence. He notes that transformations are possible within the constant interactions of mental and body reactions if we understand a process for achieving results. We know the brain retains memories of incidents that occurred in our developmental years and it is the initial shock of emotional or physical trauma that we are reacting to. It might have been a loud threatening voice that frightened us and caused a physical reaction in our stomach. Conversely, that familiar physical pain to the stomach now connects us with reliving the emotional fright of hearing a threatening voice. We reenact old retentive physical/emotional trauma reactions in response to similar situations that occur in the NOW. Therefore, any current social encounter reminiscent of your childhood trauma, can stimulate reactions to what were past traumas. Your stomach (chest, neck, shoulders, etc.), remembers the reactions to the childhood emotion of being hurt or frightened and relives those physical/emotional aches in the present. The cruelty you suffered that first time might have created feelings of self-anger, inadequacy, weakness, stupidity and more anger towards an abuser. These reactions are recycled each time you experience a similar situation in the present. You assume you can over-come these reactions, but don't know how. The *Journey to Now* can help you convert that "stomach ache" into your compassionate protector.

From Birth to Death with Sex In Between depicts my own journey to NOW, with the struggle to overcome birth issues and the stress of beginning college at age thirty-six within a troubled marriage. I received my Master's Degree in Counseling in 1983 and was inspired to create *Life Motivating Counseling*. The purpose was to help clients readily evaluate and modify their social behavior to their desired level. In time, it was the clients' validation of my sensory ability which led to the actualization of the *Journey to Now Protocol* and *Understanding Addiction*.

CHAPTER 3

Gather Your Gifts

Truth Is Felt

Sincerity, truth, enters the cavities of my soul
Through the wisdom of ages that has been told and retold,
Those vibrations of purity flow like a clean, clear brook,
Knowledge from experiences of life's existing book
Infuses my energy path, cleanses my being
Opens my electric pathways, encourages seeing,
Untruths, twisted messages, words that hurt, destroy purity
Produce electrical signals that warn with surety,
Sincerity, truth enters the cavities of my soul
Through the wisdom of ages, being told and retold.

Ongoing parental and social misconceptions imposed upon us may be the cause of the conflicted and stressful sensations in our gut. We assume these are a normal part of our being. We become accustomed to those trauma reactions that were caused by the old unpleasant environmental functioning as long as we can remember. Unpleasant and repetitive social behavior developed from traumatic childhood experiences can be frustrating. The ability to express yourself in ways that please you, may seem impossible. These recycled behavior patterns are actualized from a distorted concept of who you assume you are, originated from imposed identities you had to endure from childhood into adulthood. You might have been told, "you are bad," "you are lazy," "you are a liar," "you are a

19

coward," "you are ugly," "you are too fat," "you are too skinny," "you are stupid," "you'll never amount to anything," "you are not good enough," and so on. Were you punished, ostracized, judged and persecuted based on skin color, eye shape, different languages, cultural dress, or economic status? These are not accurate perceptions of our real identities. The resulting troublesome social behaviors and their physical responses can be adjusted by utilizing the rehabilitating *Journey to Now Protocol*. It can guide your personal passage to a clarified and revised social interaction that is satisfying to you. The map for this adventure is designed to free and expand your ability to react to present circumstances as they are.

From Birth to Death with Sex In Between offers you a gift, the opportunity to find your own inner being and to express it as it can be NOW. You can discover what your emotional identity is once you have discarded the conditioning from childhood abuse. This protocol provides the process for experiential seeking, identifying, and living those true emotional/physical sensations that are you.

In *Overcoming Arthritis and Other Rheumatic Diseases* by Dr. Max Warmbrand, he writes about the causes of arthritis. One factor he cites is stress, creating retention of toxins that causes pain in the joints. Emotional and physical efforts to cleanse these toxic conditions alleviates the pain. This process can be viewed as a parallel to the emotional fear, anguish and physical pain experienced with childhood trauma causing toxicity. This emotional reaction affects specific parts of our bodies (which may be: the stomach, neck, shoulders, etc.) creating unpleasant or painful signals. *Journey to Now* helps us recognize the recycling of old trauma reactions in the NOW. It guides the utilization of unpleasant body sensations that are converted into satisfying social interactions when you overcome the fears, anxieties, conflicts, stresses, or depressed moods previously experienced.

We know that our complex functioning coexists with one aspect effecting another. Emotional traumas affect us physically and physical trauma influences us emotionally. This in turn creates emotional and physical counterparts. Someone who gets a stomach ache when being addressed in a loud, threatening voice is reliving the original trauma reaction in the present. The stomach ache, which is a recycled reaction, affects us emotionally. We mistakenly believe it to be connected to the present social interaction, instead of the original trauma reaction.

The chapters of *From Birth to Death with Sex In Between* relate discussions and incidents which have occurred during client counseling sessions. You might be able to identify with some of the client experiences. It could be reassuring to read about varied individuals who were able to break through the barriers of continually reliving their childhood trauma reactions. Any one of these chapters that would encourage you to begin the journey to live in the NOW could lead you to the beginning of a delightful life experience. I have included some of my own life history to illustrate pathways which inspired me to develop *Life Motivating Counseling,* the *Journey to Now* and then *Understanding Addiction.*

The protocol that is presented helps us understand how to use the reactions of old trauma and discard the recycling. It becomes possible to know and react with a real perception of the world around us at any NOW moment. This involves the interaction of our inner being and the external environment. The protocol shows us how to illuminate pathways that develop the capacity for experiencing the kind of automatic social interactions that feel comfortable to you.

Developed behavior patterns from childhood are repeated until we find a way to alter them to become less stressful and more amenable for us. The protocol's process of experiencing, understanding, accepting, loving and living your true inner being overcomes the anxiety of recycling those agonizing childhood trauma reactions. You can become aware of who you really are and how you can function less stressfully and with more satisfying behavioral energy. You can learn to judge quickly who is beneficial for your life and who is not and act accordingly in the moment. I wrote this book to help you accomplish the kind of passage from where you were to where you want to be and show how you can begin to visualize what your future can be.

If you feel anxiety, anger, bitterness, or fear with social relationships that cause you to feel stress, the *Journey to Now* can gently guide your understanding and resolution of uncomfortable reactions to your social interactions.

CHAPTER 4

My Birth Trauma

My parents were immigrants from Russia who arrived in the United States in 1913. In their homeland, they heard frightening stories about hospitals. It made my parents fear all hospitals. When my mother was ready to give birth to her first child, she asked her uncle, Dr. Maurice Caspe, to please deliver it at home. Dr. Caspe was also present when her other three children were born.

Before television, our elders would retell past experiences and new ones relating to current situations. My conception and my birth trauma were one of those stories. It began with my mother being told not to have a fourth child because of kidney problems. I was an "accidental" conception.

My mother said Dr. Caspe was concerned about the umbilical cord around my neck during the birth process. He chastised my mother for not doing what he thought she should be doing to help. He told her that she was killing the baby. Dr. Caspe removed the cord from around my neck, enabling me to breathe and saved my life. The rest of the story was that my father picked me up and kissed me before I was even cleaned and Dr. Caspe said I was the most beautiful baby of all my beautiful siblings.

I was a child who had sensitivities to my environment and was always sick. As an adult, I learned that my neck had been out of alignment from the pressure of the umbilical cord. My neck had never been adjusted. Whenever I got a cold, the infected mucus from my sinuses could not properly drain and caused ear infections. I always had sinus problems and was allergic, but that was not a diagnosis used at that time. At fourteen months, I was rushed to the hospital choking and with catarrh laryngitis. They removed my tonsils, and performed the first of five mastoid surgeries, the last one at age seven. In between surgeries, I was usually in bed with influenza and a temperature of 104 degrees. When I was a child, doctors would come to your home to examine their sick patients. A doctor stood immediately in front of me and told my mother that I might not grow up unless I was protected by a glass cage.

Mastoid surgery involves the removal of bones and tissue from the back of the ear, close to the brain. I experienced that procedure five times, so it isn't surprising that my learning problems were due to those mastoid surgeries. I was a child who was not able to learn to skate or ride a bicycle because of a difficulty with balance. I made attempts as a teenager and adult that were unsuccessful. I was often sick at home and missed ongoing instruction in grades from one through three. This made it difficult to comprehend math and grammar basics. I did complete grade school and high school, but I depended upon a strong intuitive capacity that helped me develop my perceptive abilities. Years later, as an adult beginning college, a 101 Math course was necessary for the completion of my B. E. degree. My grade was a D. I was overcome with feelings of defeat and cried to the sister who was teaching the subject at the Catholic college I was attending. She gave me a makeup test, but never told me what my grade was. It was probably an F, but she passed me with a C. This sister told me that I would be a creative math teacher, who would have compassion for children struggling with math. This turned out to be true. I taught 1st and 2nd grade children for twenty years, and created rhymes and games that helped to resolve problems in math and reading. After a school year with me, there wasn't a child that didn't show marked progress. Some children started at levels that seemed to be hopeless, but I devised individualized teaching methods that were successful. The results proved to them that they can advance. Helping children with learning problems helped me better understand and utilize math. But, it was *Journey to Now* and *Nichiren Shoshu Buddhism* that enabled me to overcome problems in all areas of my life and do better than I could have anticipated.

In junior high school, a nasty vice-principal whom all the students feared, yelled at me for my many absences from school. She frightened me, and I cried. After I told her that I had been sick she lowered her voice. That incident humiliated and scared me. I made a vow at age eleven never to be sick in bed again. As soon as I felt the beginning of a cold I resorted to whatever methods were used at that time to combat illness. I would take aspirin, Epsom salt baths, an enema and hot tea with lemon. Because of my diligence I was not sick in bed from the age of eleven until I was about twenty-three. I did have recurring sinus infections, stiff necks and laryngitis.

At age thirty I knew I could not physically survive another year living in an emotionally abusive marriage. I had developed extremely painful colitis and my stiff necks got worse. My sinus condition was so bad that I could hardly breathe. With two young children to care for and no career skills I was unable to leave that marriage. I mentioned my situation to my close friend Rhoda. She asked, "Have you had enough?" and took me to see Dr. Max Warmbrand, N. D., D. O. C. Rhoda knew him through her then father-in-law Simon Gould, who ran for President of the United States on the Vegetarian Party ticket every four years.

Dr. Max Warmbrand was a naturopathic doctor and in 1956, was one of the first alternative doctors. He greeted you warmly and guided you to his desk where you were seated in close proximity. An informal discussion followed that involved your work, relationships, environment, a healthy diet, mild exercise, nightly Epsom salt baths and deep breathing for relaxation. He emphasized the interrelationship of all internal and external aspects of our lives. The session ended with Dr. Warmbrand's chiropractic adjustment and an ultraviolet treatment. My diet became vegetarian. With this new lifestyle, my weight went from 160 pounds to 130 pounds in a three-month period. The sinuses and colitis cleared, and I no longer had those severe stiff necks. This became possible even though I was still in that stressful marriage. A healthier body was more conducive for both coping with and protecting my children and myself in a difficult situation. I survived it until I could escape.

Trauma from the physical struggle to survive my birth is reflected in my persistence to overcome problems until they are resolved. I believe this is a good trait. However, I have had to learn when to "walk away" from situations that become detrimental for me. That is when individuals who are involved, do not attempt to work out difficulties constructively. Through the years, I sought experiences that could improve my life functioning. I have been a *Nichiren Shoshu Buddhist* since 1974. I chant *Nam-Myoho-Renge-Kyo* every day. The chanting diminishes harmful functioning patterns, enabling me to become the best that I can be at any given time and to help others do the same. As it was with my birth trauma, I fight "to the end" to survive obstacles and a compassionate person is usually there to help. My great uncle Dr. Maurice Caspe saved my life at birth and Dr. Warmbrand taught me how to survive with a beautiful new lifestyle.

I never met Dr. Maurice Caspe after he delivered me, but I always felt a deep connection with him. My nephew Mel sent me his obituary and picture from the September 2, 1948 edition of *The New York Times*. Seeing it brought me to tears. Dr. Caspe was a Socialist candidate for the New York Assembly and Senate. He was an early advocate for a system of socialized medicine for those who could not afford high fees. It is an interesting modern-day parallel to Democratic Socialist Senator Bernie Sanders' determination to enact a single payer medical plan in his campaign to become President of the United States. I am proud that Dr. Maurice Caspe was a part of my life.

People related birth traumas to me and I could observe the correlation between their life experiences and a tendency to recycle those experiences. A few born with Cesarean procedures say that they don't fight hard against obstacles. A young man was birthed at home with a midwife in attendance. His first physical experience coming out of the womb was being immersed in lukewarm water. He smiled, gurgled joyfully and didn't cry. That was his life experience. Another man was born prematurely and had to stay in the hospital away from his mother for some time. He reenacts an initial feeding problem, cautiously inspecting food, resists waking from sleep and is reluctant to accept new experiences. One woman had a dangerous and turbulent birth process and life-threatening physical problems for most of her life. Another young woman's birth was physically blocked for hours. When she was born her skin color was blue and she survived with immediate oxygen. Her life is a tale of struggling to accomplish life's tasks. After great emotional and intellectual perseverance, she manages to overcome these travails. One man never really trusted women and was verbally caustic with them. Later in life, he found out that his mother never wanted to be pregnant and resented the parenting experience.

Prenatal and Birth Therapy – Healing our Earliest Wounds from Conception to Birth, by Graham Kennedy, RCST, in England, presents information on the quality of our prenatal life and the birth process that begins our arrival into the world. He shows how it may have a significant impact upon our future development. Dr. Graham Kennedy writes about Dr. Raymond Castellino, of the United States, who developed a unique approach to working with babies, children and their families to resolve traumatic imprinting that originates in prenatal life and the birth process. This includes craniosacral therapy, polarity therapy, psychotherapy, trauma resolution and birth simulation work. Prospective parents who make the effort to resolve physical and emotional issues prior to conception can expect a healthier sperm and egg to create a new life.

Cranial molding due to the birth process, if not adjusted, produces difficulties with feeding, sleeping, constant crying, colic, ear problems, squint and other visual disturbances. Later in life, other conditions may manifest including asthma, autism, behavioral/emotional problems, dyslexia, epilepsy, hyperactivity, etc.

Caesarean section births may undergo many physiological and psychological changes in a short period, imprinting a significant amount of shock into the body system. Workshops are available with Dr. Raymond Castellino, in Santa Barbara, California.

Dorothy Whitten, RN, MSN, AHN-BC, CHt, teaches mother and birth companions hypnobirthing techniques for safe and satisfying birthing through guided imagery, visualization, and special breathing. Hypnobirthing advantages can shorten the first stage of labor by several hours and more rapid postnatal recovery is experienced. It eliminates or greatly reduces the need for chemical pain killers and promotes special bonding of mother, baby and birthing companion. Dorothy Whitten and I discussed the effects of hypnobirthing on the babies. She observed them being less drowsy afterwards and calmer. The babies tended to be healthier and had higher Apgar scores. Hypnobirthing is also known as the Mongan Method and this modern practice stems from the writings of the English obstetrician Dr. Grantly Dick-Read, who developed the concept of "natural birthing" in the 1920s.

There is available information to encourage prospective mothers and fathers to experience physical and emotional cleansings prior to conception. That preparation can provide an advantage for the fetus to become a baby, a child, a teenager and an adult with more probabilities of avoiding emotional and physical health problems. Diet, vitamins, herbs and exercise are some methods that can prepare the egg and sperm to become as healthy as is possible prior to conception. *Be a Healthy Woman!* by Dr. Gary Null, PhD, with Amy McDonald, has an excellent chapter on pregnancy. It offers information on natural childbirth, midwifery, a healthy pregnancy and necessary nutrients during specific trimesters. Parents want their child to experience as few birth and health problems as is possible and protocols are available to help you achieve that goal.

The importance of discussing your birth trauma with your mother, father, or available elders in the family can support your efforts for finding constructive solutions. Becoming aware of your birth trauma details can help you understand repetitive emotional and physical functioning patterns you have experienced throughout your life. Your life functioning patterns that may correlate with your birth process can be clarified and adjusted to your needs with the *Journey to Now Protocol*.

Sam planned a "wedding like" surprise party for my parents' twenty fifth anniversary. As usual, I was sick with the grippe and was crying because I couldn't attend. My mother wanted to stay home, but Sam promised her he would hire a nurse to care for me. He told me not to cry, because my mother wouldn't go. Clockwise: Sam, my grandfather and grandmother, my father and mother, my mother's aunt and uncle, my brother, his fiancée and my sister.

CHAPTER 5

I Don't Trust

My infected mastoid bones and tissue were removed with surgery. The complications started with sinus problems that traveled to the ear. I experienced five such surgeries from the time I was fourteen months to seven years old. I do not understand why, after the first or second surgery, my mother and doctors did not take note of early symptoms to avoid another trip to the hospital. At five or six years old, I was in the hospital for the fourth time. I was now emotionally resolved to wait for my mastoid surgery. A nurse told me that my cousin Lily was in the hospital while I was there. The nurse said she would take me to visit Lily, which pleased me. She took me from my bed, put me on a stretcher and told me we were going to see Lily. We went from corridor to endless corridors. I questioned the nurse about the real destination of our trip. The nurse didn't answer. I knew she lied to me and we were not going to see Lily, but to surgery. Her lie hurt me. I cried quietly because I didn't want to be a bad patient. I was betrayed.

By the fourth surgery I was familiar with the procedure in the surgery room. The doctor, without warning, would slap an ether mask on my face. When it was rammed on my face it was a frightening experience. I could not breathe for the moment. I felt as though I was suffocating and going to die, until I inhaled the ether and passed out. I experienced that terror at a young age, but I knew I had to make a verbal deal with the nurse, even after she lied to me. I told the nurse I promised not to resist or cry if she would tell the doctor to let me know before they put the ether mask on my face so I could prepare myself for the procedure. The nurse wheeled me into the surgery room and placed me on the operating table. She said absolutely nothing to the doctor about my request. The doctor slapped the ether mask on my face and I cried.

It wasn't until I was mature that I realized why throughout my life, in anger I said, "If someone lies to me once, I will never trust them again!" It was a good rule even if it did come from trauma. At six years old, I was not able to evaluate the nurse's inability to be kind and truthful to a child. What she did was emotionally painful for me. I have done considerable work on myself through the years, but without wrath I still say, "If someone lies to me once I will never trust them again." It's a good basic rule for me to follow when judging how far I can trust someone's honesty. This involves discarding the pain of a childhood abuse and using the essence of it to protect me as an adult.

I trusted doctors, lawyers or dentists because they were professionals. The assumption was that they had degrees or titles and were supposed to do the right thing. I began to understand that they were just people who recycled their childhood traumas into adult relationships. I had to develop the courage to tell those who are supposed to be our "God-like protectors," "I don't trust you, so goodbye." Of course, that would also include plumbers, carpenters, salespeople and all other persons whose knowledge and skills we seek. It has been a gradual process for me, but I do that. I searched and found compassionate, knowledgeable professionals whose guidance I needed and could trust. They have listened to my comments and offered correlating information to me. Throughout the years, I have shared what I have learned from those professionals with others who needed that information and requested it.

Those of us who have experienced childhood emotional and/or physical abuse, should be mindful when evaluating individuals before we allow them into our personal domain. We tend to revisit familiar long-term emotional and/or physically abusive relationships we are accustomed to being involved with. This makes us feel comfortable. It's like an unconscious habit that is easier to repeat. Exercising caution can help us avoid being hurt.

Observing the social interactions of those persons we are interested in can give us specific clues as to how a relationship with them might affect us. Have you detected a lack of ethics involving verbal, financial, or career issues? Are there signs of emotional or physical cruelty they imposed upon others? Have there been instances of controlling others with devious emotional tactics that put others on the defensive? You can visualize possible interactions you may encounter with that individual in a closer relationship. These examples could help you make wiser choices. It stands to reason that the way someone treats others is most probably the way they will treat you.

Considering the complex aspects of relationships, we may not be able to anticipate the entirety of someone's specific actions and reactions. We can develop a clearer sense of what to expect generally by utilizing pre-relationship awareness. It can help us to conceptualize how we could act and react with someone. This lessens the probability of being hurt by unforeseen and stressful social circumstances. It is the unexpected kind of social stress that disarms us and lessens our ability to react in ways that are more satisfactory for us.

One way to be self-protective is to prepare for unpleasant social interaction with an acquaintance by listening to yourself in role play. You can do that by speaking to yourself if no one else is available to help. You can contemplate what someone else might say in a situation that has not yet occurred. Verbally act out with words for your behavior and for the other person. Change your reactions until you're pleased with them. You can develop a more self-protective vocabulary by practicing words that express who you are and what your value system is. Collect those phrases, write them down and/or memorize them. Borrow words from others who have learned to protect themselves socially. At first, it may be more difficult to develop comfortable verbal skills, but in time, practicing role playing can create a more extemporaneous social interaction.

Phrases You Might Find Useful:

"I appreciate your efforts; thank you for listening; I don't answer phone calls after ten-thirty PM; I appreciate your patience; I don't usually date until I get I get to know a person better; I like to discuss financial responsibilities when dating to avoid confusion."

Listening to someone's reactions to your needs, indicates what to expect in that relationship:

An Unsafe Social Situation Might Be:

Person – "Would you like a drink?" (Alcohol)
You – "No thank you, I don't drink!"
Person – "What's wrong with a drink?!"
You – "I don't drink alcohol!"
Person – "Are you chicken?!"
You – "Excuse me; I have to use the ladies room!" or "I have to go; my friend is waiting for me!"

A Safer Social Scenario for You Might Be:

Person – "Would you like a drink?" (Alcohol)
You – "No thank you, I don't drink."
Person – "Can I get you some soda instead?"
You – "Thank you that would be nice."

Getting Away from an Unsafe Social Situation:

"I appreciate your offer, concern or interest, but I'm late for an appointment." – As you're walking away.
"I'd like to stay and talk, but I'm expected elsewhere imme-diately." – As you're walking away.

"Sorry, but my friend is waiting for me." As you're walking away.

It's usually a good idea to have a buddy who would know your signals for "rescuing." You can catch someone's eye and show a distressed look on your face. It is your right to learn how to protect yourself.

When You Do Feel Safe:

"Thank you, that suggestion for getting together sounds like a good idea. It could be interesting."
"I'm not able to now, but I would like a raincheck for your invitation." – While you exchange contact information.

The *Journey to Now* guides the client to recognize current physical reactions that originated from childhood abuse. These physical signals indicate the presence of someone or something in your current environment that has the potential for causing emotional and/or physical pain or pleasure. This enables you to make an instantaneous decision to leave a troublesome scene or stay in a pleasant one. The consistent practice of the protocol enables you to develop an ability and desire to stay and confront an unpleasant situation. Your reaction to it doesn't have to display anger, but you can approach it with firmness. The goal would be to change an irritating social situation and bring it to a conclusion that is acceptable to you.

You are right not to trust blindly. There isn't any need to feel guilty or bad for not trusting. You might have been hurt countless times. You have the right to be cautious. You can become more observant, more thoughtful and more skillful at being socially self-protective. Imagine yourself as a prizefighter and learning techniques with which you can defend your body. As a prizefighter, you would study your opponent. You want to know your challenger's strengths and weaknesses and how you can overcome them. With that knowledge, you could develop your ability to protect yourself and WIN! Why not win the battle to become the kind of person whose judgment you can rely upon and trust, through the *Journey to Now* experience?

CHAPTER 6

Does Change Scare You?

Abusive childhood trauma reactions are recycled into adult relationships. The interplay of those personal connections was taught, practiced and are familiar to the aggressor and the victim. All areas of functioning of sleep, work, creativity, love and sexuality are affected.

Two people with that victim versus aggressor tendencies are attracted to each other and can make all kinds of promises to entice and solidify the union. It follows that it is often the man, (but it could be the woman) who soon imposes emotional and/or physical pain. The woman who is hurt tells him she is going to leave. He promises her that he will never act that way again. He begs her forgiveness and buys her something she wanted. The woman relents, stays and they have intense "make up sex." After a while the man's abuse escalates. He inflicts more intense emotional and/or physical pain. This time, the woman, makes a stronger determination to leave. The man begs more ardently for forgiveness and he buys her something more expensive that she longed for. The woman again relents. She stays, and they have even greater "make up sex." The ongoing abuse will escalate to the point where the woman may be seriously injured or killed. Emotional pain may intensify that makeup sex experience for the female victim. The male abuser's reaction to the power he has over the victim can also stimulate his sexual behavior. A hospital visit, a religious organization or law enforcement will offer intervention from an accredited crisis counselor who can persuade the woman to leave. The promise of a professional safe house offers a sanctuary which can promote the confidence to leave an abusive relationship. Calling 911 for help can lead to information about local women's groups with safe

houses that may offer opportunities for re-education, careers or immediate employment. You can search in your area for local women's groups
or other organizations for the guidance you require.

Why doesn't she leave of her own accord? Survival fears are a reality
which may be due to financial limitations and not having safe housing for
herself and her children. The abused woman learns specific behavior
patterns for self-protection in a threatening situation as a way of maintaining that physical place for herself and/or her children. The price for
this "security" may even include the woman and her children being hurt
emotionally and/or physically. This can be all that the victim can do to
maintain a "home" at that time. The victim may realize that it is her
defensive behavior pattern which is responsible for maintaining limited
security and that could give her a sense of achievement. It's a frightening
aspect for her to even consider changing her methods. She has learned
how to live with abuse and thinks she can survive in some way. Some of
her behavior strategies may be the catalyst that provokes even more
dangerous reactions towards her. Protective behavior mechanisms
develop because of continual childhood abuse. This pattern becomes an
"addictive" syndrome for survival. It provides a secure feeling when we
can anticipate what the familiar threatening action/reaction result will be.
The continuum of sexual abuse in a young life becomes the adult's attraction to sex that is emotionally and physically cruel. The survival reaction
would be to submit to avoid other punishment.

The Journal News article of October 18, 2015 *"Leaving an abusive
relationship a complex process"* is by Danielle F. Wozniak, the Dean of the
School of Arts and Sciences at the College of New Rochelle and the
author of *Surviving Domestic Violence; A Guide to Healing Your Soul and
Building Your Future.* She writes that leaving a violent relationship is
complicated, involving love, family, violence and finances. It is a back
and forth process of wanting to leave and being pulled back by financial
necessity, fears of increased violence, or being influenced by an act of
kindness or an apology. She notes that women who are in a violent

relationship can contact Womens-Shelter.org, or the National DV Hotline at 1-800-799-SAFE (7233) for help.

In 1983, I was a qualified Crisis Intervention Counselor for the Rape Crisis Service at Planned Parenthood. I worked with sexually abused women. There was deeply felt pain, anger and fury recounting their childhood plights. Their anguish was a product of sexual betrayal and sexual violence usually perpetrated by family members who violated them instead of protecting them. Related story after story of these tragic childhood traumas were heartbreaking to listen to. It was interesting that one woman who was sexually abused by her brother felt no anger towards him. She understood his need to feel safer by bonding with her because they were both living in a threatening family situation.

There was a pattern of substance anesthetization to counteract pain. A woman brought her boyfriend who was in his forties to her therapy group. He related his experience of being sexually abused by his mother from his teen years into to his adult years. This man, as well as some of the women in the group, had become addicted to alcohol and/or drugs to escape pain and some attempted suicide. There were those who could overcome their addictions through psychological and/or drug rehabilitation.

The encounter with this group was the first time I heard the term survivor. One woman who was married and had children was still furious with her mother. As a child, she would come home late from school to avoid abuse from her father. When she finally did come home late, her father took her into his room for "punishment" and abused her with sadistic sex. She screamed but her mother never investigated. This woman's fury was that her mother "just continued to peel potatoes." This woman "survived" but with great anger, especially towards her mother, whom she hoped would have helped her.

A woman spoke about herself as a teenage foster child who needed a home. She was taken in by a professional couple as a "mother's helper." She was uninformed about her body functions and assumed her ongoing vaginal bleeding was due to menstruation. With maturity, she realized it was a result of being raped by the father daily. She never complained because she did not want to upset the mother or the children she learned to love. She was a captive in a home that she longed for and was afraid of destroying that situation. This girl graduated from high school and found work to sustain her financially and ran away. She was conflicted about leaving, fearing the father would start to rape his daughter in her absence. Each painful and furious word she spoke was an arrow of hate directed at that rapist. It pierced my heart.

Strengths

Abusers and victims have
Different kinds of strengths.
Abuser's strength is in
Controlling someone else.
Victim's strength is learning
Survival and escape.

Those women and that man went through years of sexual abuse. The emotionally and physically injured were left to cope with sadism, emotional pain and no one to confide in. The abuser usually imposed secrecy by making threats of physical harm to the family if the contemptuous acts were revealed. Children should be able to assume that they are protected by a family of loving caretakers. They feel great anger at the betrayal of family members. The pain of physical abuse conflicts with the sexual gratification that some young victims experience. It is disturbing and confusing. This has its effect on future love and sex issues, accompanied by emotional/and/or physical pain. In the 1940s and 1950s when these recounted incidents occurred, there was no general awareness of these kinds of situations. Those individuals who were abused experienced it as being shameful and secretive. School personnel or specially trained counselors were not available to help these unfortunate young people. These children had no way of seeking constructive compassion. Considering these obstacles, the women and this one man I encountered SURVIVED. It was the origin of the term SURVIVORS for those who overcame childhood sexual abuse. These people were "damaged" in the sense that they still had various levels of anger and fury inside of them. They did attempt to live their lives as best they could.

On July 23, 2015, an article appeared in *The Journal News*, entitled: *"Daughter Hurt by Mom's Failure to Defend Her."* During her childhood, a fifty-year-old woman was sexually abused by her adoptive father. Her mother caught them in the act. The next day they acted as though nothing happened, but he never abused her again. She confronted her mother recently, to discuss the incident. The reaction was silence. This daughter has a deep ache in her soul and doesn't know what to do about it.

At the time, I was working at Planned Parenthood and had not yet developed my *Life Motivating Counseling* or the *Journey to Now Protocol*. I know now that it would have helped to release and lessen emotionally destructive pain these group participants experienced since childhood. It could have allowed them to survive by redefining and living personal and social relationships less stressfully. However, in February 1984, I did call Representative Benjamin A Gilman, who was on the Sub-Committee Investigating Human Resources in Washington D.C. His letter in response to my concerns about child abuse, along with the subsequent U. S. Congressional bill on child protection appears at the end of this chapter. Our efforts can produce some results that can improve circumstances in people's lives. Just keep trying.

Those of us who have experienced emotional, physical, or sexual abuse in childhood carry its effects into adulthood. The childhood pro-grammed fear and stress become adult emotional addictions. Learning to act and react to anticipated danger was the norm. Our behavioral proto-cols were developed from that premise without any social guidelines. It can be likened to trying to cross a street crowded with moving cars and no traffic rules. One must get to the other side to survive. You may learn how to function, running in between cars safely, but sometimes you get hit. Stress and pain can become too much to cope with and drugs can take you out of that turmoil temporarily. That solution creates other problems. In Dr. Gabor Mate's book, *The Realm of Hungry Ghosts*, he writes about childhood abuse leading to adult chemical abuse.

Both men and women can be abused in intimate relationships. They may have coped with that kind of emotional and or physical environment throughout their lives and developed defensive mechanisms for daily survival. In attempting to feel safer, the woman can cry for pity, scream, or use sex as a distraction. These are attempts to delay or prevent more abuse. The man can try to fulfill the woman's demands that may be punitive or demeaning. When he's too pained, he might resort to alcohol or drug usage or respond violently.

Established and repetitious habits (behavior, food, drugs, etc.) are difficult to break, even though they may be causing emotional and/or physical pain. We choose to maintain these patterns of functioning because we are accustomed to the action/reaction it creates. This constant familiar experience gives us a feeling of comfort from knowing what to expect. Changing any facet of those "addictive" interactions creates a fear of consequences from unpredictable reactions. Envisioning the unfathomable produces a more intense anticipation of danger than the actual pain we might experience.

If someone who is kind, generous and loving offers a stable relationship to someone who has been hurt over periods of time, that abused person would most likely feel uncomfortable. That person has not created a behavior pattern to cope with the good stuff and cannot comprehend how to react to kindness. The confusion, when confronted with the unknown factor of compassion, is like being put into a dark, dense forest without a compass. Although this relationship is not abusive, the victim continues to act in ways that anticipate the old punishment from this caring person. Those reactions can be detrimental for that relationship.

The *Journey to Now Protocol* offers a specific interactive structure which can alleviate the fear of change that is involved when contemplating a caring relationship. Old trauma reactions become adjuncts to help us avoid stressful conflicts in the NOW. The more proficient we become in using them, the better they help us function more skillfully. The ultimate purpose is to experience more comfortable reactions in the HERE and NOW.

One such guide is a gentle and specific step by step structure.

1. Pinpoint the original trauma.

2. Recognize your emotional/physical reactions when you were experiencing that trauma.

3. Acknowledge that it is only your reaction to that trauma you recycled throughout your life.

4. Learn how you can utilize those emotional/physical reactions to that trauma, to protect yourself in the present time.

5. This guidance is offered to you to try to avoid the conflict, fear, anxiety, and stress which makes it difficult to make positive changes. You can learn to recognize, accept, love, and live who you really are.

I applaud your courageous efforts for beginning the journey towards allowing more joy into your life.

On her wedding day, the sunshine in my daughter Lyn's face didn't foretell years of emotional stress. I warned her, but victims have the tendency to "not see" the negativities. This can also be called a "repetitive energy functioning pattern" or karma.

BENJAMIN A. GILMAN
22ND DISTRICT, NEW YORK

COMMITTEES
FOREIGN AFFAIRS

SUBCOMMITTEES
INTERNATIONAL OPERATIONS
ASIAN AND PACIFIC AFFAIRS

Congress of the United States
House of Representatives
Washington, D.C. 20515

February 8, 1984

COMMITTEES
POST OFFICE AND CIVIL SERVICE

SUBCOMMITTEES
INVESTIGATIONS
HUMAN RESOURCES

SELECT COMMITTEE ON
NARCOTICS ABUSE AND
CONTROL
RANKING MINORITY MEMBER

CHAIRMAN,
TASK FORCE ON
AMERICAN PRISONERS AND
MISSING IN SOUTHEAST ASIA

Ms. Marcia Caspe
11 Sherman Street
Spring Valley, New York   10977

Dear Ms. Caspe:

Thank you for your recent communication expressing your interest in programs to prevent the sexual abuse of children. I appreciate you taking the time to share your professional experience as a counselor and school teacher with me.

I want to assure you that I share your deep concern that prevention programs be established and maintained for the prevention, identification, and treatment of the sexual abuse of youngsters. The vicious cycle of the abused becoming the abuser will continue until the public is properly educated and information is made readily available as to the causes and affects of child abuse. Because the sexual abuse of children is a form of child abuse, it is often included under the general title of child abuse. However all of the programs to which I refer offer services for sexually abused children.

I contacted the New York State Federation on Child Abuse and Neglect on your behalf. I am enclosing the information forwarded to my office by the Federation on Child Abuse and Neglect and hope that this information is of interest to you. Should you need more information regarding specific programs in the Rockland County region, please contact Mr. Dennis E.A. Lynch of the Rockland County Alliance for Children Task Force. His address is 11 South Highland Avenue, Nyack, New York 10960. If after you review these materials you have any further questions or thoughts on these programs, I hope that you will share them with me.

I am pleased to inform you that the House recently adopted H.R. 1904, the Child Abuse and Adoption Reform Act of 1984. As passed by the House, H.R. 1904 authorized $30 million for Fiscal Year 1984, with a 5% annual increase in authorizations through Fiscal Year 1987, for child-abuse prevention programs. I am including a summary of this legislation so that you may review the provisions of specific interest to you. The Senate version of this legislation, S. 1003, is pending consideration on the Senate calendar.

Another piece of legislation which should be of interest to you is H.R. 3635 the Child Protection Act of 1983, which was adopted in the House on November 14, 1983. This bill substantially increases the penalties for the sexual exploitation of children and prohibits the distribution of materials exploiting children. H.R. 3635 is pending consideration by the Senate.

PLEASE REPLY TO:

WASHINGTON OFFICE

DISTRICT OFFICE
44 EAST AVENUE

DISTRICT OFFICE

DISTRICT OFFICE

DISTRICT OFFICE
32 MAIN STREET

Ms. Marcia Caspe
February 8, 1984
Page 2

As a co-sponsor of H.R. 3635 and The Family Violence Amendment to H.R. 1904, I will continue to work to see that our children are protected from abuse and exploitation and that services for these children and their families be adequately maintained so that education and rehabilitation can be provided.

Thanks again for taking the time to set down your thoughts on this important matter with me. Should you have any further comments that you wish to share on this or any other matter of concern to you, I hope that you will not hesitate to contact me.

With best wishes,

Sincerely,

BENJAMIN A. GILMAN
Member of Congress

BAG:ly
Enclosures

H.R.3635
Latest Title: Child Protection Act of 1984
Sponsor: Rep Sawyer, Harold S. [MI-5] (introduced 7/21/1983)   Cosponsors
(101)
Related Bills: H.R.3062
Latest Major Action: 5/21/1984 Became Public Law No: 98-292.

SUMMARY AS OF:
3/30/1984--Passed Senate amended.   (There are 3 other summaries)

(Measure passed Senate, amended)

Child Protection Act of 1984 - Amends the Federal criminal code dealing with the sexual exploitation of children. Increases the penalties for the sexual exploitation of children from $10,000 to $100,000 and, on a subsequent conviction, from $15,000 to $200,000. Sets a fine of $250,000 for organizations.

Prohibits the distribution of materials involving the sexual exploitation of minors even if the material is not found to be "obscene."

Eliminates the requirement that persons distributing such material in interstate commerce do so for purposes of sale.

Raises the age of a minor to include any person under the age of eighteen.

Redefines "sexually explicit conduct."

Permits authorization for the interception of wire or oral communications in the investigation of such offenses

Requires the Attorney General to report annually to Congress on the prosecutions, convictions and forfeitures under this Act.

CHAPTER 7

Anger

"John" had tremendous anger. The emotional/physical cruelty he had experienced from his mother made him feel he was always wrong. He recreated behavioral situations that reenacted those hurtful experiences. At the onset of therapy, he would express the rage he had for his mother towards me. He anticipated my angry retaliation that would make him feel wrong and bad. That didn't happen, so his antagonistic behavior towards me gradually ceased. John was divorced, with a young son, and his feelings about his mother "figure" had been transposed to his ex-wife.

One day John had a visitation with his son. He carefully tucked his son in a stroller and wheeled him into a department store. John stole merchandise and carefully tucked it into the stroller next to where his son lay. He was apprehended outside the store by security personnel. He cried and begged in fear of the child's mother finding out what he had done and taking away his visiting privileges. The security personnel let him go with a warning. And he was able to keep this incident from his ex-wife.

This client didn't understand that he was recycling trauma reactions from the scenarios with his mother, which would anger his ex-wife and endanger his visitation rights. He was reliving the volatile exchanges with his mother which always ended in his punishment. The Journey to Now guide helped him understand how he was recreating his old traumas in the present. He began to change his relationships by clearly seeing the reality of situations as they occurred in the NOW. He was no longer just reenacting the painful reactions from the past. He became much more relaxed and confident controlling his behavior. The pleasant environment he created within himself, influenced his social interactions.

Anger is an emotion we experience for several reasons and on various levels. It is a basic reaction to being intentionally hurt emotionally and/or physically and may vary from slight to intense. A friend may not like your new car, which may be annoying. One family member can use a demeaning word or phrase to describe what he or she thinks you are, or someone could purposely hurt you physically. We could become careless with our personal safety, resulting in emotional and/or physical injury. We might observe an injustice when a person is being punished by having their legal rights taken from them without cause. And any one of these issues can create reactions from being perturbed to feeling rage.

You may feel uncomfortable, conflicted and/or dissatisfied with your habitual social behavior conditioned by old traumas. Attempts at changing these social interactions might have been discouraging without a specific guide for successful change. The *Journey to Now's* goal is to adjust conflicted social behaviors into pleasant ones, utilizing distressful physical trauma reactions. One former client, for fear of being hurt, hid inside her closed, self-constructed environment. While using this guide, she felt safe enough to open a door of her "box" and plan her outward journey. *From Birth to Death with Sex In Between* presents various clients' successes to encourage your participation with the guide, formulated to help achieve your desire for pleasurable social interactions.

This process illuminates the cause and effect of a traumatic emotional experience interacting with the physical, causing sensations which can be momentarily painful. Any one thing that is done to you, or that you do to yourself, effects every part of your being. Enduring pain changes the chemical balance of the body, which in turn effects the nervous system, emotions, the brain and behavior. Your behavior patterns that sustains the emotional/physical distress in immediate social interactions effects your work, love, food, family, friends or sex. This experience promptly focuses on old trauma reactions and activates an awareness of how it is possible to modify behavior reactions in a short period. The guide focuses on a review of your needs and wants. It sustains the realization that we may no longer have to live with fear or anger. You can learn to feel safe, find self-love, know who you really are and what influences your social interactions. You can develop spontaneous behavior that eliminates former uncomfortable patterns of socialization and choose intimate, social and career relationships that are beneficial for you.

CHAPTER 8

Their Unsafe Childhoods

Anorexic clients are wary of food that causes them to relive painful emotions and physical sensations. In therapeutic sessions, they tell us what they are experiencing. "When I eat the food, I feel the pain of when he was hurting me." "I hate food she always made me choke on." "I feel the pain of him so strongly when I eat the food. I have to force myself to vomit that pain out of my body." "I only take a tiny bit of food at a time, because these small pieces don't threaten me as much." "When I drink alcohol or smoke pot, I can relax and eat anything and everything. It feels so good to feel full and enjoy the food. Afterwards, I feel so guilty and force myself to vomit."

It is the related painful experiences that children endure which makes us aware of abusive parenting. Children protect themselves from the anticipated anguish of reliving those imposed emotional and/or physical pain by creating "safe houses."

Dr. Alice Chase, Doctor of Osteopathy, who wrote "*Nutrition for Health*" in 1959, in which she details her alternative methods of caring for clients, had an informal conversation with a patient whom she said had an "eating problem." Dr. Chase suggested that the patient should eat alone in a relaxed environment and not allow the abusive person to prepare her food, or even be present when she was eating. "Eating problems" at that time, were not considered to be dangerous. In the 1980s, that was called anorexia, and it is now a more prevalent problem, with serious physical complications and possible death.

There are children who have had to learn how to live with fears of ongoing emotional and/or physical punishment from parental abuse.

Stress and anxiety are components of the pressure from the vicious cycle of repercussions. A parental behavioral pattern which inflicts pain causes some children to develop aggressive physical reactions towards the abusive parent. This reactive behavior can become a catalyst for even more child abuse that can escalate to murder. Hopefully, there would be corrective intervention at an early stage of that intensified interaction.

One possible cycle of abuse is an experience of being intentionally hurt with an immediate reaction to harm the abuser. But the fear of responding entails the prospect of a harsher punishment. That trepidation can become a pattern for reactions to other social relationships. In the attempt to protect ourselves, we can withdraw into an emotional cocoon. An alternative is to become verbally and or physically aggressive to keep people away from us.

Anorexics tend to build walls of protection around themselves and create their personal "safe houses," which are complicated defense systems. Detailed and specific time blocks for eating, sleeping, school, work and exercise, are often put onto actual graphs. The anorexic develops and utilizes definite time periods to avoid anticipated disputes and anguish in their environment. In this controlled world, the anorexic designates every moment of planned and timed activity in their daily life. In their "safe houses" they feel protected from frightening emotional shocks caused by aggravating and threatening family arguments over behavior, finances and concentration on food. These defensive mechanisms affect every area of their environment, including relationships, school, work and recreation. It takes a high level of intellect to construct and meticulously micro plan these "safe houses."

Childhood's Lonely Hallways

Childhood's lonely gray stone hallways
Confusion, fear, silent cries says,
"Find me, see me, hold me, lead me
From the cold maze and darkened screams.

Free my being, so thoughts can fly
Arms and legs can move quickly by
Joy can burst out from my center.
Can you rescue me, my own mentor?
From my lonely gray stone hallway
Where confused fears, silent cries stay."

Anorexic children anesthetize themselves with drugs, alcohol and low weight to avoid emotional pain. Comments about relieving stressful reactions, "I love my weight being below average. Now, I don't have the energy to feel the stress of my life. That's a relief!" "The more I exercise, the more relaxed I get. I'm so fearful of gaining weight, because then I'll start feeling the fear of danger and stress in my home." "The thinner I get, the better, because if people can't see me, they can't hurt me." "I jump rope hard to make sure I'm burning calories it helps me get that painful food out of my stomach." To negate the capacity to feel, they run, race walk, or count how many taps each foot makes (per minute) while sitting. In therapy sessions, I have suggested to the anorexic client the use of low impact exercises such as chi-gong, yoga, race-walking and swimming for the client to avoid injuring weakened organs and bones.

Children are experiencing a lifetime of emotional pain from parental verbal, physical and/or sexual abuse. The abusive parent can create pressure with consistent verbal harassment, limiting the child's choice or quantity of certain foods. Sexual abuse, family arguments, financial and mealtime upheavals are painful environmental issues from which anorexia can develop. The media's portrayal of the desirability of thin women is also an important factor which can encourage anorexia. Women in commercials, actresses and young models with tall, very thin body structure, tell girls and women that these bodies can attract success-ful and famous men who live the glamorous life that will make them happy. It is rare, but models with fuller body shapes are finally beginning to be represented in magazine and television commercials. In the article *"A Digital Attack on Body Image,"* by Marcela Rojas, which appeared in the

June 1, 2014, edition of *The Journal News* depicts how social media supports anorexia and bulimia, encouraging this potentially dangerous body image with web sites such as, #thinspogram, #thighgap, #bonespo. We do see photos of personal recovery and histories of #edrecovery, #ed soldier, and #foodisfuel, which can encourage those who are in need of it. For help with this problem, organizations that can refer local services are National Eating Disorders Association – www.nationaleating disorders.org, National Association of Anorexia Nervosa and Associated Disorders – www.anad.org

Parents who observe dramatic weight loss and fear the possibility of the anorexic child's demise, may exert verbal or physical pressure on the child to eat more. It is difficult to modify anorexic behavior patterns unless parents (or guardians) are involved in a professional treatment plan coinciding with that of their children's. Understanding their role in creating the troublesome atmosphere which fosters anorexia is an intense process. With parental cooperation, the anorexic child is better able to modify behavioral patterns.

Some children may be fearful of hurting their parents if they tell them their true feelings. Children can be frightened that they could be rejected as a result. Issues of being lesbian, bisexual or gay might be hidden. They could also be afraid to let parents know they think that they are not capable of being part of educational or social goals they are expected to fulfill. These and other kinds of situations may be too stressful for children to hide inside of themselves and cope with. When they stop eating, their energy is depleted and the pain they cannot handle is lessened.

A client who was terrorized throughout childhood found it difficult to talk. She was careful to avoid verbal participation and any behavior which could invite punishment. Her family misinterpreted her social persona and called her the "perfect child." She lived into adulthood striving to fulfill the "perfect child" label to avoid emotional and/or physical punishment she feared. She became anorexic. She drank alcohol, smoked marijuana to relieve stress and maintained "perfect" by excelling both in school and relationships.

At eighty-five pounds, she began the *Journey to Now Protocol*. Her food selections and the amounts have increased, as did her weight to one hundred pounds. She is learning to be imperfect, with less stress and fear. She understands the origin of the "perfect child" syndrome, how she perpetuated it and is attempting to consciously overcome it.

See Me Through My Eyes

See me through my eyes
And don't ask me why
I feel what I do,
I don't think like you,
See me through my eyes
And don't ask me why
I did what I did.
It's nothing I hid.
Please see through my eyes.
Someone told you lies.
My pure heart you must
Love and know and trust.
See me through my eyes
And don't ask me why
You can't feel my soul.
To keep our love whole
See me through my eyes.
You can't ask me why
You expect me to
Walk your line with you
So don't ask me why.
See me through my eyes.

Clients verbalize histories of emotional suffering. The commonalities they cite are a lack of safety caused by fear of parental verbal, physical and /or sexual abuse. The combination of fear and food is prevalent. Clients describe a concentration on foods by an abusive parent. "She made me crazy with don't eat this, don't eat that." "As soon as he said I gained weight, I had to go to the bathroom and vomit out the pain he made me feel." These disclosures illustrate ongoing emotional and physical correlations with childhood trauma.

A young anorexic woman missing menstrual cycles, with no sexual desire said peers made her feel inadequate when they discussed their own desires. It created an emotional conflict for how she was supposed to feel. Generally, the anorexic feels more comfortable without sexual desires. Getting emotionally and/or physically close to someone can involve a fear of getting hurt that does not feel safe.

The tragic story in *The New York Times* on December 30, 2010 reported on the death of an anorexic model named Isabelle Caro. She died at the age of twenty-eight. Isabelle's weight at the time of her death was unknown, but in 2007 she weighed sixty pounds and was five feet four inches tall. In her memoir, she described a tormented childhood in which her mother isolated her. She kept Isabelle out of school until the age of eleven and forbade her to play with other children. Her mother criticized her for being too fat. Isabelle spent her life wanting to make her mother happy by striving to maintain the childhood body that her mother admired.

Family violence shocked a child who perceived the situation to be a threat to her life. The trauma made the blood rush to her face. To keep her safe a family member put a hand over her mouth to prevent her from crying or screaming and rushed her away from the scene. Into adulthood her face became red whenever she faced danger. Since the initial shock her speech was almost inaudible unless she was angry and shouted obscenities. She also had some problems with pronunciation. With *Journey to Now*, she became adept at protecting herself socially. She learned how to tell people what her needs were and what she expected from them. She said that this made her feel more fulfilled and she "felt safer." The facial redness rarely reoccurred.

A client whose stomach was hurt in a traumatic childhood situation, suffered extreme stomach pains into adulthood when she encountered emotional threats. Another client, who as a young child said something that inadvertently caused violence, developed a "closed throat syndrome." This person was afraid to speak honestly and/or loudly, and her throat closed when she experienced fear. It's so difficult for the anorexic client to verbalize the pain that is held captive in the "closed throat." One client felt guilty and fearful when trying to talk about people who wounded her deeply. With this protocol, she began to feel safe to talk out her pain and was able to bring her voice to an angry yell. At the end of the session, she said that her body felt calm. At our next session, the client said that she was more relaxed and able to function socially on a more open level.

The anorexic child can be afraid of speaking out, especially when feeling terror. The "closing" of the throat prevents the child from defending itself verbally, avoiding possible retribution. The fear of parental punishment for speaking out seems to correlate with the fear of eating. Taking food into the body that is offered by the abusive parent is equated with taking pain from that parent. Verbal skills for "speaking from the heart" are practiced by communicating one's feelings with the *Journey to Now Protocol*. Letting others know, "That hurts my feelings," "That scares me," "That makes me anxious, so please don't do that," "Thank you that was very helpful." Those persons who honor our feelings are the ones with whom to cultivate relationships. Those who do not honor our feelings are persons we should avoid (as much as a child can). A goal of *Journey to Now* is for the client to be able to judge the differences between "villain" and "hero" more realistically. It is a primary lesson for expanding self-protective coping mechanisms for social interactions. Self-protective skills are developed by referring to the emotional/physical reactions to persons or incidents in the NOW.

An extreme and consistent feeling of not being safe is a vital aspect in the development of anorexia. In one instance, there was a lack of structure in the family. A divorce complicated that non-structural atmosphere.

The mother became depressed and non-functional and the child became the angry parent. Visitations with the father and his companions made for a more pleasant situation that contrasted even more so with the mother's lack of structure. A sudden and unpleasant ending to those pleasurable visitations combined with money arguments brought the child to a state of near-death due to weight loss. By experiencing the *Journey to Now* and *Life Motivating Counseling* the adolescent was ready to walk out of the "mental box" in which she was hiding for safety. She even made plans for future schooling.

Money is often used as a form of combative control between parents, especially those with divorce issues. This intensive conflict effects the child and creates yet another overwhelming anxiety. A teenage client described herself as a child reacting to conflicts about money. They created an anticipated visualization of hunger, homelessness and no clothing to protect her from the cold and social ostracism. She worried that a threatening money situation could make food scarce. "The anger inside of me is so strong when my father doesn't give my mother money for food. How can I eat the food when I feel this deep painful anger toward my father? He doesn't give money for that food that I can't even eat. I even hoard food, because my father may not give my mother enough money for food. There may not be any food at all."

Anorexic children feel ill at the sight of food they perceive can cause pain. The stomach aches and feels "full." A sickly feeling moves up from the stomach to the closed throat. Food becomes the enemy to be guarded against. Parents who are agreeable to becoming a part of the counseling create a safer environment. The result promotes the lessening of emotional and physical tensions in the stomach, chest and throat, allowing more room for food. A client attests to the progress, "I think I'll try a hundred more calories a day." "I'm learning to bring food and eat it more calmly at school." "I'm tired of living in this box, I'm tired of worrying about the next day's food and I want to start living in the here and now."

Life Motivating Counseling focuses on the client's descriptive verbalization of immediate emotional pain and behavior adjustments. The *Journey to Now* guides the client's awareness of correlation between the emotional and physical pain or joy. Dr. Gabor Mate referred to that emotional/physical connection in his book, *When the Body Says No*. He reminds us that the mind/body is connected by the nerve and blood systems. At the beginning of each Journey to Now session, relaxing breathing techniques are used to more readily enable us to tune into our emotional/physical reactions harboring old traumas. The protocol's breathing techniques help a client relax and enables a gentle verbal re-enacted tracing of original trauma incidents. It vividly demonstrates the correlation of physical reactions to emotional experience. This breathing helps the client recollect the origins of similar emotional/physical reactions to those that are recycled in the present. The protocol guides the client to develop conscious realizations and verbal expressions of the trauma sources. It helps the client more clearly recognize how those past addictive behavior patterns are recycled now. Reeducation begins with what we can do to change that repetitive pattern. Being part of that emotional/physical connection reinforces the realization of being capable of controlling our social interactive behaviors.

The *Journey to Now's* concentration on experiential understanding evolves into behavioral changes rapidly. At each session, the client is encouraged to recall the correlation of negative or positive emotional/physical reactions to people in immediate situations. Guided by those physical reactions the client learns experientially how to choose, avoid or transform social interactions beneficially. Trust is an important issue. Clients learn not to feel guilty for distrusting certain people in their environment. Instead, they learn to trust themselves by taking time to successfully observe the validity of any individual prior to opening their "hearts" to them.

The abused child is accustomed to coping with the parents' abusive behavior pattern. The tendency is to be emotionally drawn to familiar stressful relationships. The *Journey to Now* guides the client to verbally describe and recognize the emotional/physical interaction of recycled behavior, avoiding repetition. This pattern is akin to an alcoholic who is no longer functioning as an alcoholic. There is always the danger of that "first drink." It takes time to improve and to feel secure with the changes. One can develop skills which automatically protects them from interacting with another abuser.

Results of this therapy with anorexic clients are very rewarding, especially when parents who take part adjust their behavior. The anorexic client begins to feel safe enough to be more verbally forthright with parents, siblings and in general social situations. They begin to expand their limited environmental "box." The process of peeking out of it for safety before they walk out can occur as rapidly as within three to six months with the combination of *Life Motivating Counseling* and the *Journey to Now*. Clients can identify and live their true inner beings and pursue advanced education, careers of their own choosing and satisfactory relationships.

Young people who have been reacting to threatening parental stimuli throughout their lives often freeze in response to social anxieties. To counteract that tendency, it is important that clients are experientially educated to acknowledge and utilize physical symptoms of an aching stomach or closing of the throat developed with childhood traumas. These sensations can warn them to avoid threatening persons and/or situations they encounter as best they can. The anorexic person can attempt to verbally negotiate distressful situations as they become emotionally stronger. They can learn to develop and utilize a beneficial freedom of choice in all aspects of life.

Anorexic clients have had the courage to explore their pain, verbalize it and reeducate themselves for a better journey through life's future. Observing clients initial deeply felt and painful responses and the progressive actualizations from work with the *Journey to Now* is very moving. It's an intense rescuing protocol which empowers the client. Anorexic clients want people to know of their pain so that others can be helped. They have described medical difficulties involving kidneys, the heart, the digestive process, osteoporosis and a lack of menstrual cycles.

The destructive emotional and physical aspects of anorexia are depleting. It is important to create safe childhoods. The goal of the protocol is to help ourselves to help others.

Courage and Bravery

Can one blow away the thick fog
That obliterates road vision
When pursuing speed, direction?
The addictive, emotional
Childhood patterns create
Intense hurt from reenactments.
Encountering source of fierce pain
Can build courage to clear the paths
For new emotionality,
Fulfilling one's own true seeing
Establish one's own true being
Living one's true reality.
Hearts sing observing bravery
That creates joy from misery
While blowing away the thick fog
That obliterates road vision.

CHAPTER 9

Parenting and Grandparenting
Through My Eyes

In 1968, I took a two-week summer vacation to Ocho Rios on the island of Jamaica. We rented an efficiency apartment at the hotel. We chose to do that because it was such a delight to shop for our own delicious fruits and vegetables at the marketplace and buy freshly caught fish from the waterfront.

Jamaican women would rise at daybreak and gather fruits and vegetables to sell in the Ocho Rios marketplace. Their children also rose early, to be ready for the trip with their mothers. Their clothes looked freshly washed and ironed in preparation for the journey.

I noticed young children were relaxed and playing quietly by themselves or with other children. One three-year-old boy sitting at his mother's appointed area created a game. He whispered directions to a large clove of garlic as he moved it around. I was impressed at how calm and comfortable this child seemed to be.

My vacation ended, and I returned to my 1st and 2nd grade students in a suburban New York school. In my classroom, I noticed the difference between the physical reactions of young Jamaican children to those from New York. Some of my children were restless and easily distracted during the required quiet sitting time for completing reading and writing tasks. This behavior continued, although we had fun throughout the day with short physical activity periods of dancing, exercising, running in place and deep breathing. This was planned to complement the learning process and counteract the effect of young children sitting for long periods of time.

The Journal News article of September 9, 2015 entitled, "*Students Learn to be Mindful,"* points to breathing exercises that are used for relaxing and to encourage listening to oneself and one's environment. Based on Jon Kabat-Zinn's Mindfulness-Based Stress Reduction, learning to be in the present, reduces stress and fosters better focus and learning for students. I am delighted that the breathing exercises I initiated in the 1970s are currently being used in school districts.

I lived six blocks from the school where I taught 1st and 2nd grade from 1968 to 1988. In later years, it was not unusual to meet former students who recognized and approached me, although I was not familiar with what they looked like as adults. It was twenty-five years after my 2nd grade class presented my musical play *"Birds Do It,"* which comparted bird families to our own. At that time, I was waiting for a refund at Home Depot and noticed the birds that were nesting in the ceiling rafters. I discussed that with the woman in charge of the department. She said, "I thought you looked familiar. I was in your bird play and it was really good." Another student stopped to tell me that he was in an international finance Master's program and another one was studying international languages. One student waved at my car and said, "Remember me? I was the baddest kid. You were the only one who got me to be good, because you gave me peanuts." Students remembered and related specific things I taught them. They don't forget teachers who are sincere, honest and caring.

Our assistant principal at South Madison, Barbara Ragsdale, believed that every child could learn, and she searched for programs that would stimulate individual needs. Our principal, Gerald Buchhalter, facilitated programs to bring our low-income neighborhood school averages to equal other more upscale districts. Their efforts helped to fulfill our vision for what the children's future could be.

There are differences in cultures, climates and economic conditions which effect children's behavior. Jamaican children's diet during the 1960s, contained a great deal of locally available tree fruits and backyard garden vegetables, herbs, grains, with some goat meat, fish, or chicken. They consumed much less refined sugar, chemicals and salt, as compared to the average American child's diet. Dr. Gary Null's documentary DVD, *The Drugging of our Children*, refers to the effects chemicals have on children's health and behavior.

Food and its effects on the emotional and physical wellbeing of the children was an important issue for me. Each day at school I included a mid-morning snack time. I initiated discussions with the children as a means for them to express their ideas about different foods. The children said, "health foods" were good for you and "junk foods" were not. They said, "Junk is something you throw away and don't put it in your stomach." I encouraged the children to bring healthful snacks from what was available at home; fruits, vegetables, cheese, hard eggs and leftover chicken. I joined them while eating my fruit while we had informal food "chats."

At the neighborhood school where I taught, a good number of children walked to and from school each day. Some parents brought them to school in the morning and picked them up at the end of the day. It created a community feeling when the parents and I could exchange necessary comments about their children each day. It was known in my school building, that I ate healthy foods. Parents who wanted to eliminate sugary foods from their child's diet were glad to discuss this with me. They were happy to send healthier cupcakes and juices for birthday celebrations. These same parents and I discussed the hot lunches, including the desserts, that were freshly prepared for the children in the school kitchen at that time. I made them aware of a double-blind design with an experimental protocol that reduced sugar from school diets and had a positive effect on behavior. The research data entitled *Diet and Crime* by Stephan J. Shoenthaler, PhD, was a study of 279 incarcerated juveniles who were given a reduced quantity of sugar in their diet and the result was a 71% improvement in positive behavior over a two-year period. With behavior and health on our minds, the parents accompanied me to the principal. We suggested better choices for hot lunches. The principal, who was mostly concerned about behavior, was made aware of the research and he cooperated. Sugar was replaced with honey. Fresh fruits and raw salads were included with each meal.

I purposely created a pleasant classroom environment for the children, so any contrary behavior was a concern for me. Fortunately, Halloween only happened once a year. The children brought treats with high sugar content for the annual party. Parents could not find an alternative at that time. After my first Halloween party, I noticed an immediate change of behavior in twenty-six first graders. It was as if there was an immediate reaction to some "hyper pills." Twenty-six children acting out en masse was not a safe situation. My defense before the next Halloween party began was to have the children pack their belongings for home before the party started. When the party was over, the children picked up their belongings with enough time to walk to their school exit. This enabled them to run off this excess energy on the way home. This avoided any behavior problems that might cause injuries in the small confines of the classroom. In time, some mothers became aware of available tasty treats that were healthier. By in large, Halloween was and is still largely a "sugar-time´ and with hyper active behavior.

My son Lee was born in 1946 and my daughter Lyn in 1953. Through the years various parenting trends were suggested. There was breast or bottle feeding totally in response to a child's needs, or those determined by schedules. Child/parent relationship philosophies varied from physical nurturing without parental behavior guidelines to structured behavior guidelines combined with physical nurturing.

Your Birth

Having maternal bulge
And beating grateful pain
Pierced by the greeting cry
Of your young hungry mouth
Taught me divinity.

My first child was born before I was twenty years old. I had not studied methods of child care. My initial responses were influenced by my personal reactions to my child's individual needs. There was a structure for bedtime, mealtime, bathing and dressing, with "open-ended" nurturing. The first child behavior book I read was *Play Therapy* by Psychologist Virginia M. Axline. It helped me understand how I could create fulfilling verbal exchanges with my young son that were supportive of his creative pursuits and relieved emotional stress. As he grew, I wanted to understand the general variances of his emotional and developmental needs that correlated with age differences. Jean Piaget's theories of progressive stages of a child's development were particularly informative. As time passed, I developed responses to my children's needs as they grew, to help them become the best they could be for themselves. I combined intuition, knowledge and truth in my search for a better understanding.

After completing my B. E. degree, I became an elementary school teacher. Parent/teacher conferences with report card signing were scheduled bi-monthly. Parents were often surprised when I described their child based on their satisfactory functioning in my classroom. That behavior was not always what they experienced with the same child at home.

My classroom protocol was based on behavior modification. Rather than chastising children for inappropriate behavior, verbal praise and some token rewards were bountiful for appropriate behavior. The students focused their attention on me because they wanted positive guidance for attempting to fulfill their assignments and being praised for the completion of those efforts. It was a pleasant, functioning classroom.

The classroom traffic protocol was specific. The children lined up to walk into the classroom in one direction and walked out of the classroom in another. They walked from one assignment area to another in routes that avoided confusion and confrontation. The children welcomed the basic rules that were consistent. They knew what was expected and how to achieve necessary goals. This allowed more energy to be devoted for thinking and learning without negative distraction. Creative activities involving art, music and storytelling were included in all subjects. Individuality was encouraged.

In a classroom averaging twenty-six students with three reading levels, some of which were problematic, each small group moved quietly to prescribed centers or to work at their seats. This allowed for more individualized attention. There was hardly any negative behavior during this transition, because each child was eager to complete assignments for me to check and offer favorable comments for their efforts.

In *Behavior Modification, the Human Effort* edited by Robert H. Bradfield, in the chapter entitled *The Engineered Classroom: An Innovative Approach to the Education of Children with Learning Problems* by Frank M. Hewett PhD, Frank D. Taylor Ed. D, and Alfred A. Artuso EdD, the authors note that it is important to create work areas in the classroom in which students can achieve educational goals. Children progressing from one assignment area to the next without confusion and with successful completion reduces negative behavior. This encourages learning and lessens the frequency of behavioral problems. I found Dr. Haim G. Ginott's book *Between Parent and Child* to be informative and constructive in the classroom, as well as at home with my children. Addressing a problematic incident rather than focusing on personalities avoids disciplining from anger. When the child spills milk, rather than telling the child that he/she was clumsy, stupid, or not paying attention, just ask the child to get a sponge and clean up the spilled milk. It teaches the child responsibility for personal actions at home and in society.

There was a movie about a horse whisperer and a television program about a dog whisperer. The trainers showed how they became the "lead dog" or "lead horse." In other words, they were in charge of developing acceptable behavior. Who else should be in charge if not the responsible guardian? The child must learn to talk, walk, use the bathroom and learn how to interact with people in their social environment. The parent is the teacher. Influenced by the child's individuality, the parent can guide the child to recognize necessary social, ethical and moral rights and wrongs.

The parent teaches the child to function in all areas that are necessary for personal survival. Socially, it is important to learn to say please, thank you, to respect those adults who are trustworthy and to tell parents which adults or peers are threats to him/her.

Contemplate what would happen if the child is allowed to make and break basic family rules and regulations in the home at one year, two years, or seven years old. If those children are to be "in charge" at a young age, how will the parents be able to guide the eleven, twelve and older teenage child to not choose drugs, sex, or violence? It is the parent who teaches the child to become self-protective and live non-violent lives.

It is not surprising that children grow into an adulthood that reflect their childhood experiences. A child raised with fear becomes a fearful adult, one who is abused becomes an abuser, one who experiences cruelty becomes cruel to others. Given kindness he becomes a kind adult.

Children thrive on endless love, acceptance and support, enabling them to evolve into who they are. They need consistent family structured rules that are fair to help the child know what to expect from adults and how to react. This allows the child to feel more emotionally secure. In that environment, the absence of mentally/and or physically conflicted stress enables the child to utilize more energies for growth and discovery. This helps them better understand who they are and how that relates to the world. A realistic and fair family structure becomes the behavioral pattern the child transfers from the family to society without confusion. This enables them to apply energies that are free of mental and physical stress for positive development and to produce constructive pursuits which can be directed towards the world they live in.

Grandparents are an important part of the family and can influence the child's social growth. Grandparents are no longer young parents whose energies are concentrated on nurturing their special partners, maintaining their homesteads, rearing their children and finding some personal time. They can now focus on the privilege of playing games, reading books, singing, dancing, initiating creative projects and introducing our grandchildren to an extended world of nature, people and culture.

A visit to the grandchildren and their family should involve following their home rules. Grandparents are not the parents. Child rearing suggestions can be offered diplomatically (or not at all) depending upon the relationship with the in-law parent. Emergency care decisions must be discussed with parents (if that is possible) when grandparents are caring for the children.

The role of a grandparent can be cultivated within the existing family unit. It is a delightful opportunity to become a pleasurable asset and enjoy devoted little grandchildren. They become companionable teen-agers and doting adults that can brighten our senior years.

A variety of economic and legal circumstances make it necessary for a growing number of grandparents to become surrogate parents. They rescue their grandchildren while relieving their struggling children of basic child care. These stalwart grandparents can earn their grandchildren's love and their children's devotion.

The joys of grandparenting are there for you to experience.

I was fortunate to have shared lovely outdoor explorations with my granddaughter from birth to her pre-teen years. Recently I gave her the following poem I wrote for her when she was younger. Lily is now an adult. She continues to enjoy the beauty of nature and is moved by her memories of wonderful childhood days with her grandmother.

Lily In The Woods

Lily finds adventures in the woods
Searching high and low as Lily could
Up in the sky she sees an airplane,
A bird is flying, singing its name,
Maple seeds have rabbit ears and eyes,
The ants run quickly as they rush by,
Bees have their lunch on flowers yellow,

With sticks and rocks Lily finds some ground holes,
Kitty cat runs away through the trees,
"Get you" game can catch Lily with ease,
Daddy Long Leg does walk so fast,
Frogs can jump up, up, up as they pass,
Lily finds adventures in the woods
Searching high and low as Lily could.

I met Aunt Florence when we worked in the same company to earn extra money. Aunt Florence became the kind of mother that I longed for. She was eighty-five and I was fifty-four. She had been a music teacher in South Carolina. Her minister husband died and her nephew sent for her to move to New York and live with his family.

She and I shared a room on a training weekend with the company we worked for. I went to a far corner of the room to quietly do my morning Buddhist chanting. Aunt Florence said, "Darling, that sounds like lovely music. What is it?" I told her that it was my morning prayers. She said, "Teach it to me and we'll sing it together."

I would call to take Aunt Florence to the movies with me and to local events. I was always happy to greet her on her unplanned visits to my home. She took me to her African American gatherings and to the home she was now living in with her nephew.

We would chat about everything and were supportive of each other.

I told Aunt Florence I was going to the Village Vanguard in New York City to listen to jazz. She was interested and accompanied me. The famous jazz drummer Elvin Jones was appearing. She loved the music and said, "This Mr. Jones looks like he's one of the Carolina Joneses." I said, "Let's ask him." After the performance, we approached Elvin and she posed her question. Elvin Jones winked to me. He wanted to please this lovely grandmother. He said, "I suppose I could be one of the Carolina Joneses."

One day I said, "Why couldn't you have been my mother?" Aunt

Florence said, "Darling, I never had children of my own and you are my daughter and I am your mother."

Modify, change and improve your own life pursuits. That in turn effects everyone around you, including children, other family members, work associates and intimate relationships. Congratulations for making the effort to better understand and implement new knowledge in your life process with the *Journey to Now.*

My son Lee thrived on love and peace during the first two years of his life, when we were alone most of the time. But, with the divorce, came years of turmoil.

Into adulthood, my granddaughter Lily continues to feel serene when she is close to nature's beauty.

CHAPTER 10

Our Family Dynamics

I was hurt and angry with my family in my teenage years. It was my nephew who gave me the opportunity to review old family dynamics and a new in-depth history.

I hadn't seen my nephew Melvin in thirty years. We did speak when his father passed on in 2011. The reconnection with my nephew was important, because we really got to know each other for the first time. In 2012, he contacted me because I am the last surviving senior relative who could offer him historic information about our families. Melvin has a profound interest in learning about our lineage. His computer searches were very thorough and included steamship passenger logs going back to 1913. I suggested that he focus on the Caspe family, because they're so interesting. I was very moved when Melvin sent me a history of Dr. Maurice Caspe's life. He was born in May 1859 and passed on August 31, 1948. Melvin enclosed Dr. Caspe's picture from an obituary column in the *New York Times* dated September 2, 1948. I realize now that Dr. Caspe might have known Simon Gould and Dr. Warmbrand because they were perusing similar social concerns in the same period.

In my family, three siblings all married and left home when I was twelve years old and I became the only child. There was little communication between myself, my parents and my married siblings who were busy with their own lives. I realize now that was when I became my own parent. My lifestyle developed differently from my family and they did not accept it. This created more of a disconnect from them. The pictures and data Melvin sent me and our discussions rekindled memories of warm family connections from my early childhood that I had forgotten.

In particular, I had special feelings of belonging with the Caspe family. They were creative individualists, social activists and family oriented. I felt akin to them.

My social behavior developed differently from that of my siblings. It is said that each new child is born into a different family unit, with modified family dynamics. This changing unit is influenced by the location and conditions of living quarters, parental relationships, number of siblings and their ages, presence or loss of grandparents or other relatives, pets and financial conditions. Various combinations of any of these factors exist as a new sibling enters the family unit.

How individual family members react to the new baby affects various inter-relationships and the entire family dynamic. The mother may be tired or ill and may have to delegate baby responsibilities to an older child or the father. The baby may require intense physical care, leaving less of the mother's energy for the father and the other children. The baby may be so adorable that the mother may over indulge affection not given to the father and other children, creating jealousies. Or, this very lovable baby can make everyone dote on it and share this additional joy between them. Adding to the mix, the father can be helpful, destructive, or simply avoid the entire situation. The consequences of these and other possible scenarios influence the newborn and other siblings. They begin to assume individualized roles in the family. This becomes a social continuum.

There have been instances when I was fortunate enough to be invited to a client's family dinner. It was very informative for the progression of the life-coaching process. The family eating together reveals relationship attitudes in a more extemporaneous manner. The various behavioral patterns for choosing certain foods, how it is chewed and swallowed, begins for the newborn when nursing or being bottle fed and then moves to solid food. These first feeding experiences involve early emotional contact with the mother, father, siblings and other family members. They become the basis of emotional relationships associating food consumption with those family members. These emotional connections seem to become more obvious when social barriers that control behavioral pretenses are more relaxed as the family eats together. The observation of the client in the "family food habitat", or in the company of companions, can be helpful for the counseling process. It certainly can be an interesting experience for anyone who may be considering a closer relationship with a member of a family or peer group.

When contemplating a personal relationship with a member of a family one can easily observe who is dominant, who is angry at whom, who is helpful, who is victimized and how these different attitudes interact. We can see how the person, in whom we are interested in, acts and reacts in this family, or a group of friends while he is dining. These observations can give us important clues about how the kind of relationship he has with his/her family or friends can affect us and our future life with him. Will you be stressed, fearful, happy or peaceful with that person? With this knowledge, you can visualize what could be a pleasant relationship, or you can decide to discontinue the relationship. These contemplations help to determine who you will allow into your life. In times past, elderly women would caution younger women to see how a man treats his mother to know how he would treat his wife. This also holds true for how a woman's relationships with her father affects the relationship with her husband. When we think of those issues it helps us understand the behavior of a "person of interest" more realistically. This can avoid emotional upheavals in the future.

Group therapy is an option for reevaluating one's association with your own family. Hearing different family members relate their versions of the same story offers you a better understanding of the interactive behavior patterns within your family unit and how they originated. This relevant information can help you comprehend your own involvement in the family. You can reassess your behavior in that family and how it affects your general social behavior.

The *Journey to Now's* protocol provides additional tools for you to reevaluate learned childhood behaviors and how you relate to adult social interactions. A purposeful reconstruction of those behaviors can become what you desire them to be.

The adventure is yours to pursue.

The family in 2014: My granddaughter Lily, me, my husband Manny, my son Lee and my daughter in law Kathy.

CHAPTER 11

A Love Relationship with Ourselves

Emotional Refugee

I am searching for my own true home
So my heart will not be alone
Where the joy of singing love's song
Vibrates cavities to belong.
The environment can surround
My emotions that seem so sound,
But uncertainty, agony,
Acceptance rejection of me
Trying to become a part of
Communities with the hearts of
Those that will mask souls to fit in.
Who, what I am, how can I win
The battle to test my courage.
Pain from loss can well discourage
Discarding masks and finding me,
Being, winning, for all to see,
Living my own identity
Is by far the whole entity.
I was searching for my own home
It's in my heart that is not alone.

LOVE can be an emotion we feel for someone, with general expectations of it being given back to us the same way we have given it. We experience love for different reasons, in many ways and within various kinds of relationships. There are interactions with a companion, with our family, with a sexual partner, with a parent, with our social community and the world. Behavioral functioning is complex and totally individual in any one of these social situations. Why do we feel a specific way about a social interaction? Why doesn't someone else exhibit feelings exactly as we do? Individual behavior patterns are developed by parental relation-ships and family dynamics. These are models' children adapt and recycle into adulthood with their families, friends, acquaintances, work associates and romantic partners. Those family patterns children retain become social attitudes, involving love, kindness, physical and/or emotional cruelty.

Behavior patterns some parents expect from their family, a vision of what their offspring should be, can be different from who the child really is. Some children live their lives fulfilling parental concepts of who they "should be" to feel safe or to earn parental affection and praise. Living someone else's dream can lead to an inner sense of something not being right. That conflict creates stress and self-doubt between what we are taught we should be and for not developing that someone we really are. We don't always understand or are able to define this conflict. It sends us mysterious messages from within our gut that makes it difficult to know how to eliminate that inner discord. That unnamable, incompatible gnaw-ing is like a restless embryo that was supposed to become you, but has not yet been able to be born.

The *Journey to Now* can guide you to the location of that embryo. It enables you to become familiar with it, nurture it, love it and give it life. Having done that, you can give your true being a gift of parenting. You can become the master of your choices, differentiating between the ones that are constructive or destructive to your life. With more confident perceptions, you can begin to behave in ways that complement your being. Even if you were to make a choice you become displeased with, you have the option to change that decision. For example, you have the freedom of saying, "I have given this matter a second thought and THIS is really what I want to say or do." You have the freedom to proceed with your preference.

In the *USA Today* article entitled *"They Said What"* of April 28, 2015 Kim Kardashian talked about her stepfather Bruce Jenner's decision to identify as Caitlyn. She said that it is hard to live your life being one person for society and someone else inside. If Caitlyn is happy living her life being who she really is, then Ms. Kardashian is happy for her and supports her 100%.

Our lives are affected by parental, educational and basic societal rules. Socially, moral and ethical rules guide our behavior. Societal rules are necessary to prevent someone from hurting another person, for safe driving and preventing theft of money and property, to name a few. Each additional social rule or relationship involves factors that are imposed upon us from outside of our internal environment. They can add stress to already burdened emotional and intellectual confusion. This protocol that is offered to you can help you facilitate what your special needs are for individual behavioral success while discovering who you really are. Dr. Gary Null's book and DVD *Who Are You Really?* give examples of different life-energies (Dynamic, Adaptive, Creative, etc.) and is an excellent adjunct for self-discovery.

The Unresolved

What I am not
To me I cannot
Be to you or
Anyone else.

The primary focus of the *Journey to Now* is on our relationship with ourselves. We question our reactions to internal and external stimuli and we get answers. Are you pleased with them? Are you conflicted? Are you hurt? Are you angry? The protocol guides efforts to develop automatic adjustments for social actions and reactions that please us. The goal is to respond to our external environment with instantaneous clues that avoid insecure feelings and emotional conflict. Less stressful responses help us feel safer and more satisfied without worrying about what our behavior should be. This protocol guides social reactions that can eliminate emotional toxicity adapted from our grandparents, parents, school and society.

We may interact socially, utilizing developed behavioral conflicts we have become accustomed to. It is easier to go along with a habitual functioning pattern that can result in a complex and confused self-image. These reactions are ingrained within us and we begin to believe we are really hurt, angry, or a negatively aggressive person. Less effort is involved maintaining our disharmony and incompatible social behavior than seeking our true inner being. We feel comfortable with the familiar strife we are used to. We may do this to avoid punishment for not living someone else's concept of what our life "should" entail. It is not easy to discontinue habitual behavior without specific guidance for constructive change. An anguished sense of conflict can be the catalyst that leads us to the *Journey to Now*, or a therapist for help to unravel that unpleasant, complex emotionality.

The protocol promotes awareness of self-identity by encouraging the client to recognize interactions of emotional and physical responses. It fosters the eventual mastery of automatic social responses that are complementary to our true inner being. We can feel comfortable with who we really are without the conflicted stress that was part of each social interaction. We can learn to function more confidently, utilizing those old and burdensome physical responses to create a new and wonderful journey. We are the only ones who can identify our internal roadmap for exploration. With a newfound freedom and a new energy flow, relaxing and playing becomes more readily enjoyable.

The basic premise of *Life Motivating Counseling* therapies which include the *Journey to Now Protocol* and *Understanding Addiction* is to gently discover the core of one's conflicted confusion and learn who one really is. The big prize is to recognize, love and live the true you.

CHAPTER 12

Choosing Your Relationships

Chasing Butterflies

We may chase those elusive butterflies
White, brown, yellow that fly low and up high
Who flutter their wings as they pause to rest.
Their flirtatious beckoning is a test
To challenge the chase without proper net
That makes final catch unattainable.
Then one day one knows how impossible
It is to catch dreams without proper tools,
That is when we cease acting-out like fools
And stop chasing elusive butterflies
White, brown, yellow that fly low and high.

Eighteen-year-old "Angie" feared one parent's anger and she was anxious about displeasing the other parent. There were arguments about money. This young woman recycled her trauma reactions socially. She chose to marry someone her mother favored. Angie thought he could offer financial security and he might be responsive to her emotional needs.

Angie was functioning through her trauma reactions and hadn't yet discovered who she really was. She wasn't totally aware of what she was longing for. She didn't know how to ask her husband "Jason" for something he didn't offer. Angie didn't realize how important love and compassion were for her. She shared sports with her husband, but he was not interested in her sculpting, singing and alternative healing. Sex was not fulfilling, and the relationship did not satisfy her real needs.

Angie did not have a clear vison of what her life's goals were aside from raising her children and managing her household. Jason knew that his role was to fulfill the family's financial needs. He took part in some sports and enjoyed eventual financial success that made luxuries and special vacations possible. The death of his abusive father caused emotional confusion. He became involved in an ongoing sexual relationship with a co-worker. Angie discovered the affair and was furious.

Angie began *Journey to Now* sessions and Jason participated in two of them. She exhibited fierce anger due to his betrayal and he was not willing to discuss his behavior. Jason did not accept financial responsibility for his family after he left the home. A difficult divorce made it possible for Angie to receive an acceptable financial judgment and Jason had liberal visitations with his children.

Angie continued the protocol sessions and discovered she had competent financial and creative abilities. She pursued an educational path to discover a personal career for helping others. Angie is interacting socially in the reality of NOW, rather than through recycling trauma reactions. She is looking forward to being part of a romantic relationship. Angie can now choose with an awareness of her identity and the ability to share emotional and physical companionship.

Jason did not continue the protocol sessions. After the divorce, he made extravagant financial decisions that caused a monetary decline. Jason did not sustain his parental obligations and lost the trust of his children. Their telephone and social contacts became fewer as the years passed. In time, Angie's personal growth enabled her to reestablish and redefine her relationship with Jason from being foes to being friends. She encouraged him to rebuild his relationships with his children who are now adults.

Finances, career, recreation, relatives, location of homes, planning and caring for existing or future children are all issues that should be evaluated before getting deeply involved in a relationship. Conflicting life-style values and choices can create insurmountable relationship problems. It is important to observe and discuss a prospective partner's needs and issues and evaluate how it relates to yours. One partner may be concerned with saving money for unforeseen financial problems. The other may be stimulated by spontaneous purchasing of items or activities which are momentarily exciting. A solution to any potential challenge between value systems should be mutually acceptable and a specific plan should be established and followed. When discordant preferences in any area of a value system causes anger, arguments and frustration, that stress can lead to the demise of the relationship. Love doesn't always conquer all, it must be nurtured.

A recreational choice for one partner may be football, while the other favors ballet. One option may be for both to attend football games and ballet together. An alternative could be to accept a situation where each partner attends their choice of recreation individually. Showing an interest in and/or joining someone you care for in their recreational pleasures becomes a "round-robin" with that partner responding in kind. Efforts to please one another are appreciated by those who are sharing recreational fun. Conversation that is respectful of each other's ideas is a key for finding a mutually acceptable method of compromise. Taking part in each other's preferences can be amicable, but one must be wary about participating in any activity that is harmful to you and violates your value system. If you feel uncomfortable, think twice about developing a closer relationship with that person.

Challenges in a relationship might involve two individuals from varied cultures and/or family value systems that are different. It is important, when resolving problems, to find common ground that is acceptable to both partners in any kind of a partnership. Do we reject the other person's preferences, or do we listen to the other person's point of view? Do we respect differences if they do not offend our sensibilities? The major point is there always will be problems to resolve. Some of them are fun to work through, some are difficult, some are big and some are small. An important factor in maintaining a successful and lasting relationship depends upon finding a mutually conducive method to resolve problems. The key is HOW we choose to work out conflicts successfully.

Before you decide who you will allow into your life, observe a prospective partner's ethical and moral behavior with associates and family. Don't trust instantaneously. It can save a lot of heartache and prevent precious time lost and a waste of your resources. Honor that true inner being you will discover with the *Journey to Now*. The experience can help you learn to respect the wisdom of using your body's sensations as you react to people and incidents.

"Arthur" married a woman he loved. They struggled together through college in the early years. A lack of finances made it necessary for them to live in a sub-standard apartment. They maintained a loving and caring relationship. In time, with college behind them, they achieved their goals for successful chosen careers and social status. This couple purchased a home and they had a son shortly thereafter. Everything seemed to proceed towards their socially acceptable plan for a better life. But, somewhere along the line, they lost the closeness of those early days. And a divorce was agreed upon.

Before I begin couple counseling, I ask about the good things they remember from the beginning of their relationship. Oftentimes, this helps the efforts to resolve present disputes. When reconciliation is not possible, I recall how Leonard Cohen's tender song *"Hey, That's No Way to Say Goodbye"* tried to soften the pain of an inevitable breakup. Even though I was the one to end relationships, that kind of compassion might have made a difference for me as well.

Arthur who was now single, maintained his own apartment and had regular visitations with his son. He was trying to reevaluate his life as a single father. Arthur wanted to understand who he was now and what he could be doing with his life. This newly divorced man participated in *Journey to Now* sessions during this period of introspection. He was attempting to free himself from childhood concepts that concentrated primarily on success as a means of achieving prescribed social and financial levels. Arthur still wanted a good standard of living and was willing to work for it, but he realized relationships should also be nurtured in that process. Arthur subsequently developed a balance when making decisions as a divorced male, a single father and his desire for a good life. He was finding out what was most important to him in his life.

With a clarified ability to judge his newly defined journey, Arthur considered the possibility of a new relationship. He met someone who captured his interest. Arthur was ecstatic with this wonderful woman who he said was beautiful. I met her when she visited him one weekend and his description of her was accurate. They were very much in love and married shortly afterwards.

Prior to the marriage, Arthur said that he was a little perplexed because of the similarities between his ex-wife and his new love. He was happy, and his questioning was lost in his newfound joy. The new groom had decided to retire from his previously chosen career. The woman he married arranged her responsibilities, enabling her to spend most of her time with him. There was no longer a great concentration on just building new careers. It was a promising beginning for a new life plan.

Reactions to romantic and social situations can be deceiving. It is important to delve into the connection between your behavior in the present and your original trauma. You may meet someone who excites you emotionally and or sexually. The assumption could be that this must be a good connection, but it may be a recycling of old trauma reactions.

There are different components to relationships. Some are beneficial, and some are destructive. Opposite energies are usually drawn to each other, like the north and south elements of a magnet. There are the attractions between the victim and the abuser, one who needs care and the caretaker, and a quick thinker and a slower, deeper thinker. Are you choosing someone because you are reenacting old relationship patterns? Are you functioning through who you really are in the NOW? There is a correlation between clarifying your relationship's functioning when using the *Journey to Now* and the success of your encounter.

Those who have been abused should not trust immediately. You are accustomed to an abusive relationship and feel comfortable in one, though it may be hurting in some way. Redefined information about yourself, coupled with the new relationship skills you acquire from this protocol, can develop a new social wisdom. Observe people, their behavior, their companions, their honesty and their work and play ethics. Learn to utilize your new, successful method of judging who you can trust and who is beneficial to you in your life. It's like living in a castle with a surrounding moat and a drawbridge. Lower the drawbridge to allow only those you can trust to enter your castle.

It is possible to learn how to get away from persons and/or situations that you sense can hurt you. It can become a creative endeavor to expand a socially protective vocabulary. For example, saying, "I'd like to stay, but I'm late for an appointment" and then just keep walking away. "Sorry, I had to be in 'Frisco an hour ago," or "I have diarrhea and I have to run." You can become comfortable verbalizing an immediate response to tell someone you will not accept their attitudes towards you. You have the right to say, "Please do not use that language or attitude with me" and walk away. You may decide to reconsider a relationship, only if you can observe improved behavior responses to your value system over time.

You cannot change anyone other than yourself. The attempt wastes your energy. It can be emotionally disappointing and financially draining. You can only develop your ability to discover who YOU are and learn to understand, love and live YOUR true inner being. The protocol guides the utilization of protective emotional/physical warning sensations. They alert you in an encounter with someone who rejects and dishonors who you are. You can automatically reject a relationship because of that kind of behavior. You no longer need to allow insults and negativity to invade your being. This new level of immediate reaction helps you become instantly aware of your discomfort. Actions and/or words can let a person know what kind of behavior you will or will not accept. This gives him or her an opportunity to adjust their behavior to acclimate to your new level of functioning. You have not changed the other person. You have modified the way they treat you, not who they are. When you set the standards for the kind of behavior you will accept from others, you are offering them a gift. You are giving them the opportunity to learn how to adjust their behavior towards you and become more understanding, considerate and compassionate. Some will accept that gift, others may not, but that is their problem, not yours. Move on if you are not respected. There are those who treat people with consideration and kindness because that's who they are.

My protocol gently identifies the original trauma which causes emotional/physical pain. It can help you readily discover the connection between the old emotional and/or physical trauma and its influences on your current behavior. The protocol shows us how those old emotional reactions and body sensations, developed from childhood traumas, can become our friends. They can protect us from persons or situations that may cause anguish in the NOW. That evolved perceptiveness makes us more aware of those safe pleasurable emotional/physical sensations developed from childhood experiences. They too are recycled in current social situations and are just as important as the unpleasant ones.

The *Journey to Now Protocol* can clarify how your childhood trauma and reactive sensations affect behavior patterns NOW. They become guides that can protect you. You can recognize, understand and trust the connection between your emotional/physical reactions and the beneficial experiences. It takes practice to know and live the true you. Your skills can progressively improve with repetition of a newly acquired self-guidance. Life is a learning process and the protocol utilizes your childhood trauma reactions to effect behavior patterns NOW. It can make judging who you allow into your environment become a more successful process.

You can experience immediate new understanding for your behavior interactions with this protocol. It does require your effort for continual improvement. Dr. Gary Null, PhD's book, *Who Are You Really?* is an excellent guide for learning about varied personality types and their life energies. "Natural life energy theory…a powerful tool for understanding themselves and others." The book notes three main types of people. The dynamics have charisma and an affinity for change. Adaptives are not charismatic or looking to change things. The creatives have a different kind personal rhythm, awareness and sensitivity making it necessary to bring their creations to the world. Within these broad types are the aggressives, some assertives and supportives. *Who Are You Really?* Helps you discover who you are, how you can function as an individual and with whom you could choose a more successful relationship.

The *Journey to Now* eliminates the need for using temporary band aids for unpleasant situations you can avoid.

CHAPTER 13

Our Relationship Dynamics

David Knox in *Marriage, Happiness* writes that a person knows he is loved, by the way people act towards him. What they say, how they look, how they touch and what they do. Attention, praise, and physical contact demonstrate this. Who cares if someone loves him if he never receives evidence though attention, contact, or words?

Do you feel emotionally and/or physically uncomfortable in an existing relationship? Are you contemplating becoming part of one? *From Birth to Death with Sex In Between* explores the behavior patterns of couples. You could discover how you can create a gratifying adventure. The protocol experience can enable you to differentiate between reenacting your original trauma, or freely living your true being and choosing your creativity, relationships and sexual preferences.

An important factor for any relationship success is good manners, something not taken into consideration very often. Saying "please" shows consideration prior to making a request and "thank you" shows appreciation for someone's efforts. This makes the other person feel pleasantly acknowledged. It encourages their reciprocal efforts to please you. Receiving emotional, verbal, or physical responses of appreciation are gratifying.

Pleasurable feelings effect our reactions when we make love. The other person might touch you in a way that excites you. If you respond with an aroused sexual moan or physical reaction your partner gets your message. He/she is pleased that you are sexually aroused and is physically and emotionally stimulated. He/she will remember that mutual response and repeat the same gesture. That becomes a pleasurable experience for both. If you respond to pain or show irritability, your partner should stop what was being done to you. If your partner does not stop the irritating gestures, or does not attempt to please you physically, you are in bed with the wrong person. Get out of that bed! What happens there is reflective of what happens in the living room, kitchen, etc. Sex is just a reflection of the entire relationship, involving passion, compassion, or cruelty.

Do not assume that anyone can read your mind although verbal and/or physical reactions establish an interactive code within a relationship. Your partner may not realize your need for something at any given moment. You can suggest what your needs are. "It will really be helpful if you could take out the garbage." "I'd really appreciate it if you would lower the music volume", etc. Some appropriate verbal responses for cooperation could be, "Thank you, that was so helpful." Or, "Your efforts make things more pleasant." It makes the other person feel valued for fulfilling your needs. The helper felt good about being acknowledged and wants to feel that way again. These kinds of verbal recognitions encourage repetitive efforts to please one another.

This is reminiscent of my father who didn't trust hospitals and had little regard for medical doctors. He used to say, "If you don't tell a doctor where it hurts, he doesn't know where to look." In other words, you are providing a road map with directions for any relationship. Defining a basis of what you can give and are willing to accept creates a clear interactive guide.

It is important to accept a partner's capacities. One may excel in dishwashing and the other may be an expert floor sweeper. The excellent dishwasher may expect the expert floor sweeper to be an expert dishwasher. The expert floor sweeper may expect the excellent dishwasher to be an expert floor sweeper. Assuming someone's capacity, without inquiring about their true abilities, creates anger, stress and emotional barriers. The challenges involved when trying to change someone else to be what you expect them to be can lead to animosity and ongoing arguing. It debilitates the energies of both involved. The rancor it creates is almost guaranteed to destroy the relationship. Accepting and respecting each other's capacities and efforts lowers stress levels and is more conducive for building congenial interactions.

Sharing Personal Truths

I can only communicate my truth
And express what and how much I am, to you
The knowledge coming from what I can be
Developed wisdom from what I can see
Intuitive realities I feel
Energized senses that make my head reel
Thoughts, feelings, experiences relayed
Those expressions of known truth parlayed
The energy waves I transmit to you
Share the total awareness of my truth,
This is how much I can express to you.

A premise of Dr. Haim G. Ginott's book *Between Parent and Child* can be applied to adult relationships. He wrote that in classrooms he was strict with unacceptable behavior, but permissive with feelings. However, acknowledging and accepting a partner's feeling doesn't demonstrate agreement. It only shows respect for the other person's right to have those feelings. Being strict with unacceptable behavior that may be destructive protects us from being violated. This form of self-defense can become more effective with your consistent practice of the *Journey to Now*.

Dr. Ginott's theory about focusing on the problematic situation, rather than the personality, is a more productive way of dealing with immediate matters. A vase may be accidently broken. Instead of telling the responsible person that he/she is clumsy, stupid, or not caring, one could just say, "Please get the broom and pick up the pieces." This avoids an angry confrontation. A discussion can follow to find a place for another vase, to avert a repetitive incident. Cleaning up the mess one created demonstrates guidelines, noting that those responsible for a situation are the ones who must remedy it.

It is important to develop a conciliatory and constructive method for resolving differences. A suggestion might be:

1. The two (or more) individuals in a dispute can sit facing each other for a pre-determined period.

2. The rule is for each person to be able to express their concerned viewpoint without involving personalities. An example would be speaking only to the issue. "When the toilet seat is lifted and not put back down, and I have rush to urinate, I can fall into the toilet."

3. The person being spoken to listens and is not permitted to interrupt. They remain silent for sixty seconds. The other person has their turn to present their problems in the same way.

4. After the session, remarks about the problem are presented only to declare how they intend to remedy the situation. "I will put the toilet seat down after I use it." Just the incident is discussed and NOT personalities.

At thirteen, I told my mother that I wanted a college education to attain a psychology degree. My mother refused. The recourse was a commercial high school, where I was not capable of learning stenography and math. There was no opportunity for me to develop my true abilities. I became a square peg trying to fit into a round hole. At that age, I had not yet developed a concept of who I was, what my needs were and how to choose and maintain a constructive relationship. At nineteen, I allowed myself to be chosen by a man who was not able to grow. He could not sustain his career, relationships, or fulfill responsibilities of a husband and father. I was not capable of mending that situation. It ended with a divorce at the age of twenty-three. Next, I was pursued by a man who was emotionally bitter. I was in "marriage misery" for nineteen years. At that time, my adult son Lee gave me Joni Mitchell's album, *Song to a Seagull*. She sings about not being able to go back there anymore, how her keys won't fit the door, how all her thoughts won't fit the man and that they never can. It appears she must've written that song about me. This helped reaffirm my emotional and visual concept of my relationship and made apparent the immediate need for leaving. The marriage had caused pain for me and my two children and ended in divorce.

In 1973, it seemed like I was the only divorced female living in Rockland County, New York. The following year I met famed jazz bassist Richard Davis. I watched him perform with such joy, taking part in musical conversations with other eminent jazz musicians. It brought my life into focus and I knew I had to find that same kind of feeling from my own work. It did happen for me when I taught self-awareness classes at Rockland Community College and led groups on women's groups for N. O. W. This still holds true when I observe my clients benefiting from the *Journey to Now*.

Richard introduced me to *Nichiren Shoshu Buddhism* and invited me to attend meetings in New York City. I met other Buddhists who were single, and I enjoyed "hanging out" with them on weekends. It was a delightful transition from a stressful twenty-year marriage to an exciting single life. I was now an independent woman with a steady teacher's salary, owned my home and having an exquisite time exploring the 1970s art, music, theatre, dance and single culture of Manhattan. One night, I was waiting for a seat in a tiny macrobiotic restaurant. John Lennon and Yoko Ono were leaving the only available seats. John came towards the exit where I stood. We were two Libras, wearing Granny glasses and standing two inches apart. Yoko stepped aside to allow John to greet me. It seemed like an eternity while he stood there smiling and waiting for a response. I was so overjoyed I couldn't talk. Finally, he walked out of the restaurant with Yoko and I went to sit in his seat, screaming inside of myself. All I wanted to say was, "I love you, I love your music, your humor and your peace messages."

In 1974, I became a *Nichiren Shoshu Buddhist.* Chanting *Nam Myoho Renge Kyo* enhanced my ability to see reality as it occurred in the HERE and NOW. It enabled me to visualize the *Journey to Now Protocol.* This guided my ability to stop recycling my childhood trauma. I was able to express who I really was and allowed myself to be courted by a man who has the capacity to grow personally and to respond to the needs of another in a relationship. In this marriage, we are continually evolving as individuals and as partners who offer mutual encouragement. There is much love.

Gentle Love

At the end of a stressful day
Stroke my back in a gentle way
Don't forget the rest of me too
I will reciprocate to you
Let's bond bodies close together
In warm, cold, or stormy weather
Skin close to skin and lip to lip
Joined at the head and at the hip
Joyful and playful hand in hand
We wander into slumber land
At the end of a stressful day
Stroke my back in a gentle way.

"Susan" was a client who met a "nice person" and she visualized him to be as stable as a solid oak tree. "Evan" in turn liked her enthusiastic energy in a variety of activities. He said that she brought sunshine into his life. Soon into this new relationship Susan became impatient with Evan's hesitation to partake in a variety of enjoyable things that she would suggest. This was despite her joining in his pursuits. At first Evan enjoyed her cheerful energy. In time, he felt threatened by her extemporaneous manner of pursuing new things. This relationship didn't work out. Susan realized he was too "solid" and not able to be more flexible. He said that he needed more time to overcome career problems and the effect of old relationships. It ended amicably, and they became friends because she could share her compassion, insights and successes based upon this protocol. Susan could now move on. She felt more capable of assessing and becoming part of other relationships with a clearer and more confident focus on what her needs are for successful interactions.

A goal of this protocol is to develop a more precise concept of who we are. This is especially important because we're always sending verbal, emotional and physical messages to others. They reflect our personal level of knowing, loving and living who we think we are. It involves responses that accept and reject various levels of pleasant or unpleasant behaviors of others. With the *Journey to Now*, you can choose and maintain relationships that have the potential of becoming interesting, pleasant, exciting and loving for each person involved. You can begin to live who you really are. David Knox in "*Marriage Happiness*" writes about how demonstrating verbal and physical appreciation for the "good stuff" can be a beautiful experience.

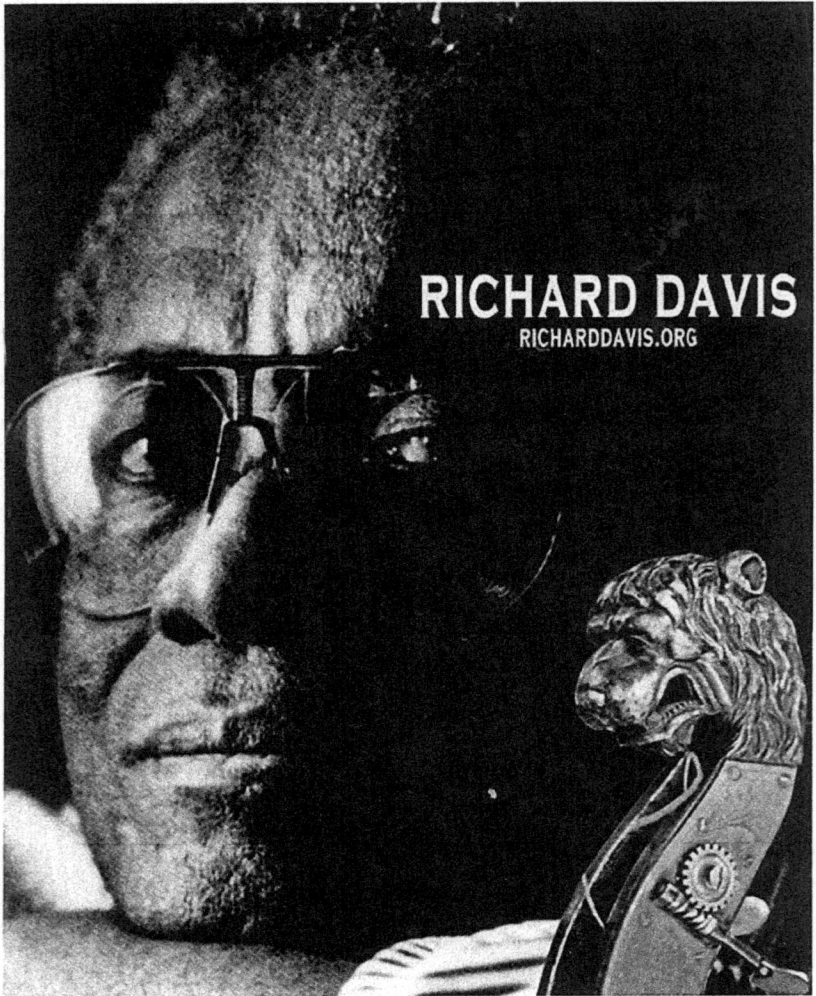

RICHARD DAVIS
RICHARDDAVIS.ORG

Master Bassist, Richard Davis encouraged me to chant, to take charge of my life and to begin a whole new phase of living in the NOW.

CHAPTER 14

Marriage After Living Together?

Why?

Why is it just your insight that can equal my own?
Why is it that it's just your body warmth can soothe my tone?
Why is it I want just you for sharing deep passion?
Why is it that our union doesn't fit into fashion?
Why is it that just you can accommodate my power?
Why is it that just you can catch my tears in a sad hour?
Why is it that your creative pursuits are like mine?
Why is it that our love-making can be so divine?
Why is it that our work does not require a distance?
Why is it that just our shared energy maintains its stance?
Why is it that your inner strength equals mine by chance?

When two people who are attracted to each other become involved in a relationship, one or both may feel an emotional and/or physical intensity, with a need to be together all the time. They may not be ready for a marriage commitment, but might feel more comfortable with just living together.

During the "courtship" period you may have noticed that the other person's good and bad behavioral attributes are affecting you emotionally and/or physically. Are compromises for ongoing issues easy or stressful? What percentage of final decisions are yours, his, or shared? How much do you trust her/his emotional, physical and financial loyalty? Do you feel hurt, or violated without being able to defend yourself? These are some elements that effect relationship patterns. Specific issues and/or your value system may harmonize or be in conflict. You may feel discomfort or stress when discussing ongoing differences. It may be difficult to find mutually acceptable solutions. If this is so, individual or couple counseling or seeking a relationship elsewhere may be advisable.

Some individuals tolerate problematic issues and avoid talking about them for fear of being rejected and/or losing a partner. Maintaining the relationship might be more important to them than the stress they are living with. If that is the case, the message sent to the partner is that though ongoing behaviors are disturbing, they will be tolerated so the partner can continue to maintain that pattern. Those interactions that are accepted prior to marriage will continue to create irritations, hurt, conflict and stress after marriage. Such a relationship will survive only as long as it can be endured.

There are those who plan to wait until after the marriage to change previously accepted behaviors that are annoying or unpleasant. They decide they can correct a particular conduct just because "we are now married." These maneuvers can be equated to getting married under false pretenses. It confuses the partner who may feel hurt, angry, or betrayed. It was assumed the relationship was acceptable "as is" prior to marriage. The person being asked to change might wonder, "What's wrong all of a sudden?" Couples might find a solution with discussions and/or therapy, while others may not.

There may be an agreement for specific behavior prior to living together or marriage. There is a possibility that one of the individuals may agree to the provisions only to guarantee the living arrangements take place, but will renege on the promises. To be sure the terms will be fulfilled, the participants could wait at least a month or two, to observe expected changes. Proving the validity of the situation beforehand is better than suffering the agony of betrayal and breaking up.

In the Beatles song, "*We Can Work It Out,*" Paul McCartney sings about trying to see it my way and to think of what you're saying. You can get it wrong and still you can think it's alright. Try to see it my way and we can work it out. This is an illustration of how not to work it out.

The following scenarios are general examples of how some people may interact in a relationship. It's a checklist of what may be important to you. Prior to committing to a relationship, these issues can be discussed for mutual consensus and may lead to a "work in progress" for successful results.

1. SOME ASPECTS OF LIVING TOGETHER

    A. Let's try it out to see if it works.
    B. No legal commitment because it can be broken up.

    1. Dissolving it does involve emotional, physical or financial hardships.

2. WHO MAKES DECISIONS

    A. One person
    B. Both cooperate

3. HONESTY

    A. Consistent
    B. Inconsistent
    C. Never

4. ASSOCIATES

    A. Observe family, friends or business associates.

    1. Good pursuits.
    2. Questionable pursuits.

5. FINANCES FOR LIVING ARRANIGMENTS

    A. Cooperative with specific responsibilities.
    B. Separate, with specific responsibilities.

6. FINANCIAL CONFLICTS

    A. Spend freely, save, invest.

      1. Discuss mutual solutions.

      2. Fear of discussion.
          a) When one individual experiences conflict and remains silent for fear of losing the relationship, the emotional undercurrents can be disturbing.

7. RESIDENCE CHOICE

    A. Own or rent.
    B. Urban, suburban or country.
    C. Discuss solutions or face emotional upheaval.

8. CAREER

    A. Educational preparation
    B. Unplanned
      1. No specific direction leads to couple's conflict.

9. FAMILY PLANS

    A. Children, how many?
    B. No children.
    C. Existing children.
      1. Discuss specific plans for residence, visits, financial support.

10. HOBBIES

    A. Choices
      1. Individual or mutual.
      2. The absence of a plan creates conflict.
    B. Flexibility for important, or less important choices

11. RECREATION
   A. Planned
       1. Discuss interests that are mutual or different.

   B. Conflicted choices
       1. Compromise by sharing each other's interests. An agreement to pursue individual interests can avoid conflict.

12.   HYGENIC ASPECTS
   A. Self-care
       1. Consistent or negligent
          a) Will partner accept hints, or can you live with the "fallout"?
   B. Environmental care
       1. Maintains surroundings.
       2. Negligent.
          a) Will a partner accept a mutual plan. Or can you live with the aftermath?

"George" and "Annette" were clients who lived together for two years while they were college students. They had communication and behavior problems, but continued to live together in "civilian life." Annette's feelings were continually hurt by verbal communication and inconsiderate behavior.

Annette experienced ongoing *Journey to Now* sessions. George wanted to improve the relationship and took part in both an individual session and two couple sessions. Annette maintained ongoing meetings and began to express more self-confidence. She accepted her partner not wanting to take part in activities of her choice. Through Annette's consistent efforts, George became more verbally and behaviorally considerate of Annette's emotional needs. They listened to each other's ideas, developed trust in each other's expertise and acted on them. After living together for seven years, the couple married with the result being an affectionate and "working" relationship.

One couple lived together prior to marriage. After marriage, "Dan" decided to shave his moustache. "Alece" was very upset because this changed her visual concept of who he was and she didn't know how to cope with it. Dan would not grow back his moustache and Alece could not accept his decision. They could not resolve the issue and divorced.

Two people lived together for seven years. After they married, the wife wanted to change the husband's behavior that she previously accepted. This created stress that had an unpleasant effect on the relationship and it ended.

The most obvious incidents of couples living together is that of celebrities, whose relationships are frequently depicted in the media. We see celebrities together for long (or short) periods of time, getting married and breaking up within a few weeks or months. Some have had very elaborate weddings. In our own social circles, it is likely that we know couples who have lived that kind of experience.

Some people feel trapped in a marriage after having lived together for a while. The decision may suddenly feel too permanent for them to accept. Sexual bonding can lessen and/or some behaviors of emotional and/or physical cruelties can manifest. "Jennifer," who was a client, had a five year "living together" relationship that involved emotional cruelty with intense sex. Immediately after the marriage, "Bob" felt trapped. He was not able to achieve an erection for three months and was emotionally cruel to his wife. Even after achieving an erection the emotional cruelty didn't stop. It ended with the wife's death due to illness. If a marriage is a comfortable choice, emotional and physical bonding can become more loving and the sexual experience more experimental.

We can observe and experience some or all the above relationship factors prior to a commitment. It is interesting that these behavioral observations are not always in the forefront of our conscious functioning. Sometimes they can be realized later. When asked, "Did you see those behaviors before?" one answer is, "I saw the problem, but I hid it from myself. I was afraid of breaking up the relationship." Another is, "I didn't want to admit it, so I hid it from myself." The experience of this protocol guides you to focus on the reality of NOW. Decisions no longer need to be based on perceiving your environment through old traumas that occurred in a previous time. This protocol helps clarify who we are and what makes us happy or unhappy. It offers a better understanding of who to allow into our lives and who to exclude. In our daily functioning, there are always good situations to encourage or bad ones to resolve. More successes and less unpleasantness are certainly goals you can learn to enjoy through the *Journey to Now Protocol*.

CHAPTER 15

Our Changing Social Standards

Industrialists controlled the economy in the 1800s and early 1900s. One such industrialist was John D. Rockefeller (1839-1937), founder of the Standard Oil Company. *The New York Times* reported in 1937 that he was accused of crushing competition, getting rich on rebates from railroads and bribing men to spy on competitors. He coerced rivals (under threat of being forced out of business) to join the Standard Oil Company.

In 1904, "muckraking" journalists wrote articles about political corruption, harsh factory conditions and unhealthy tenement slums. The government's prosecution of Standard Oil Company practices was a result of hard hitting articles by Ida Tabell. It was Theodore Roosevelt's anti-trust legislation that contrasted with those who served before him, He used government regulations and policies to protect labor unions and economic and environmental justice. President Theodore Roosevelt established the Pure Food and Drug Act and fought against unfair trading practices.

Dominant economic, political and religious powers influenced personal finances, social attitudes and sexual conduct. The Catholic Church's ban on contraception declared that sex was only to be practiced for procreation. Divorce would not be recognized. Women generally had no control over pregnancy issues. Imposed abusive relationships were a permanent trap for women within the men's overall culture of dominance.

In 1830, Joseph Smith established the Mormon Church, advocating polygamy. Mormon men were allowed to have any number of wives at one time. In 1847, his successor, Brigham Young, settled a Mormon community in Utah, which still exists. Some fundamentalist Mormon groups that hold on to those early precepts have since developed in other areas, advocating men's rights to have multiple wives. There have been recent news items of men and women who escaped from those Mormon communities. They publicly discussed physical and/or emotional abuse and the questionable practice of choosing underage girls for wives.

In the period leading to the turn of the 20th century, women had little or no opportunity for self-determination over their finances, property, political and sexual domains. Men were not giving up their control. A familiar phrase "It's a man's world," was an entrenched sentiment. The stories told by grandmothers and elderly aunts related incidents that occurred during this period confirmed that attitude. Women had few alternatives available for developing and safeguarding their economic situation. Pre-marital and marital sex were available means for women to gain financial security. These were ways of protecting themselves, their children and maintaining the family unit. Getting a husband and keeping him sexually satiated was important. The absence of a working male figure or husband made it necessary for married or unmarried women to find menial or sex work to care for their family.

There were women who strove to become a dominant force in financial matters. Transformative individuals have led movements for the freedom to work for life sustaining wages, affordable education, the decision to procreate, the choice to abort, to stay single or to marry same sex or traditional partners of choice. The Women's Trade Union League (WTUL) was founded in 1903 to raise wages and improve conditions for mostly young, single women, widows and women of color. Margaret Sanger founded the Birth Control League in 1870. This became the Planned Parenthood Federation of America. The goal was to raise the age of sexual consent, to stop sexual exploitation and the right to refuse sex in marriage.

Women's emotional, physical and spiritual beings were affected negatively by forced and abusive sexual encounters. Equal sexual treatment for husbands and wives in "compassionate marriages" improved a woman's experience. Fortunate women enjoyed sexual participation with their husbands when they could make suggestions for having their sexual needs satisfied. The reaction to that pleasurable experience was, in turn, to fulfill their husbands' desires. Married or single men in multiple sexual relationships, didn't always maintain financial security for everyone involved.

Economic independence allows women the freedom to actualize life pursuits of their own choice. There were rare females who developed their independence and assert themselves. It took almost a century of sacrifice for them to normalize financial, emotional and sexual freedom.

African American women were in bondage as slaves. When "freed" the employment usually available to them was domestic work. There were those who broke the barriers and created freedom for themselves and others.

Sarah Breedlove, born in 1867, worked in cotton fields and was the child of sharecroppers. She said that she got her start by giving herself a start. She worked hard to maintain herself and her daughter. Sarah married her third husband, Charles Joseph Walker, a St Louis newspaperman and changed her name to "Madam" C.J. Walker. She founded her own business and transformed herself into one of the 20th century's most successful self-made entrepreneurs of hair products. She became the first female millionaire. Madam Walker opened Lelia College in Pittsburgh to train hair "culturists." She contributed to the building fund of the "Colored" YMCA in Indianapolis. In 1916, Madam Walker helped fund the NAACP's anti lynching movement. In 1917, she, along with Black leaders from New York's Harlem community, presented a petition to the White House advocating anti-lynching legislation.

Ida B. Wells Barnett, in the 1890s, was a teacher who became a journalist. She founded clubs that related to health, sanitation, education, women's lynching and suffrage. Mary Church, Lugenia Burns and Mary McLeod Bethune founded similar clubs to also combat the racism that created barriers for economic independence and in turn, sexual freedom.

In 1932, Franklin D. Roosevelt became the 32nd President of the

United States. He depended upon and welcomed his wife Eleanor's first-hand assessment of the country's economic, work and living conditions. Her observations influenced laws and actions to countermand the Great Depression. President Roosevelt was the first to appoint women to positions that were unprecedented in number and rank. Among those appointed were Frances Perkins, Secretary of Labor, Nellie Tayloe Ross, Director of the U.S. Mint and Josephine Roche, Assistant Secretary of the U.S. Treasury.

After President Roosevelt's death, Eleanor Roosevelt became the first U.S. delegate to the United Nations and was chairman of the Human Rights Commission. She was respected world-wide. Eleanor Roosevelt was revered by women who at that time were trapped by their positions of wife, mother and housekeeper. My mother was one of those women. She fantasized about the possibility of accomplishing economic, humanitarian and personal freedom, because Eleanor Roosevelt had the courage to do that. The recent documentary, *The Roosevelts: An Intimate History* by historian Ken Burns, noted that her women companions felt free to express their sexual needs with other women.

Despite my mother's admiration for Eleanor Roosevelt's accomplishments, she reacted negatively in 1939 when I told her I chose a high school which would prepare me for college and becoming a psychologist. Her response was, "You must be crazy! Become a secretary and get married." She didn't experience the freedom to fulfill her own needs for a professional career that could enable her to be useful outside of the home. My mother lacked the compassion to encourage me to fulfill my needs. Instead, I completed what was then termed a commercial high school education. The instructors made valiant attempts to teach me to become a stenographer and a bookkeeper. The reality was that I was not successful with "steno" and couldn't add a column of numbers accurately. That school experience left me with a sense of inadequacy. After graduation, the feeling stayed with me. I was fired from more than one office job because I could not fulfill the requirements of the assigned work. I wanted to study psychology because I was interested in it and I knew I could succeed. My plan was to pay for my college tuition by earning money as a model. But, I didn't know how to cope with men who were "suggestive" and whose goal it was to continue touching my body and I stopped modeling.

Socially, as it usually follows, I was attracted to others who also felt inadequate. This led to an unplanned pregnancy, a hasty, difficult marriage, divorce, a second difficult marriage and a second pregnancy. It wasn't until I was thirty-six that I was able to start my college education at a new and affordable local community college. This began a long journey towards financial self-determination that made a second divorce possible. The saddest parts of this experience were the effect these conflicted and stressful marriages had on my two children. Their attempts at lengthy corrective therapies could not undo the consequences from those years of emotional pain.

I strongly suggest that young men and women try to search, study and work at careers they enjoy, as much as possible, before finalizing a relationship. Knowing who you are and what your place is in society is a better foundation from which to choose someone who will be a partner in your life.

During the World War II years, over three million women took a vitally active part in the labor force and the military. At war's end, in 1945, these women were laid off to make room for returning veterans and had to go back to being housewives.

In 1949, French author and philosopher Simone de Beauvoir wrote *The Second Sex*, explaining that women were stereotyped as being on a lower level than men. In later years, her book became an inspiration for the Women's Liberation Movement.

In 1960, President Kennedy established the Commission on Status of Women focusing on employment, social security and education initiatives to open new opportunities for financial freedom. The first oral contraceptive became legalized in 1960, lessening women's fear of pregnancy and fostering more sexual freedom. In 1963, President Johnson appointed the Equal Rights Opportunity Commission to protect women from workplace discrimination. In the 1970s, many women, encouraged by Women's Liberation, were seriously pursuing meaningful jobs and professional careers. Women were no longer financially dependent. This had an impact on relationship choices and who the sexual initiator could be.

In 1973 as a newly divorced and an employed teacher, I was accepted as a single woman who was divorced and was dating. Yet, there were "friends" who would no longer include a young, attractive "divorcee" in their social functions. I was told later that the reason for my exclusion was fear that their husbands would be attracted to a pretty and "sexually hungry" woman who no longer had a husband to fulfill her needs.

In 1963, Betty Freidan published *The Feminine Mystique* questioning whether women were happy with their marriages and motherhood. In 1966, she was among those women who founded the National Organization for Women (NOW). The purpose was to exercise all privileges and responsibilities in true partnership with men. By 1972 they supported the right to an abortion and protection for rape victims.

In the late 60s, I returned from a Caribbean vacation with a vaginal infection. I tried using my own herbs and a gynecologist's prescription without success. A friend suggested that I attend a Women's Liberation group for solutions to my problem. At that meeting, I was one of five women lying next to one another, bare-bottomed on a carpeted floor. We were each given a mirror, a flashlight and plastic speculums created by the nurses (because metal ones were cold). We were shown how to examine our vaginas to detect early irritations or infections for immediate treatment. Nurses told us that a yellow greenish discharge required honey for healing and that a white discharge required yogurt for healing. I inserted the honey for two nights with a turkey baster and lots of towels and the infection was gone. This kind of caring enough to share personal information, gave women the freedom to make valid decisions that involved the wellbeing of their bodies. For me, it was a new, safe and serene feeling to be with nurses who showed concern for correcting and preventing problems involving my female organs and offered simple solutions that worked. This contrasted with the typical male gynecologist who inserted a cold speculum, gave me a standard medical diagnosis and medication, and if that remedy didn't work it was my fault. A midwife told me that with the introduction of the birth control pill, protection against sexual disease became lax and it caused more vaginal infections, so she used golden seal douches. This was before herpes became more widespread, I tried it and it worked. I gave that information to nurses who welcomed it on a late night WBAI FM radio program and they shared it with other women as well.

It was gratifying to know that activist Gloria Steinem, among others, had the courage to publicly inspire so many women, including myself. We realized that we could activate our personal and social freedom. She was a strong advocate for the Women's Liberation Movement and co-founded *Ms. Magazine* in 1972. Ms. Steinem wrote *Revolution from Within: a Book of Self-Esteem, Outrageous Acts and Everyday Rebellions* and *Moving Beyond Words*, among other bestselling books. She helped found the National Women's Political Caucus, for pro-equality women in politics.

The "second wave" of the feminist movement emerged in 1965. Masters and Johnson published *Human Sexual Response*. Betty Dodson was a divorced, financially independent artist. This enabled her to explore her sexual freedom and encouraged other women to do the same. She wrote her best seller, *Sex for One*, in 1973 and offered self-pleasuring "bodysex" classes for fifteen years. In a 2014 interview in *The Guardian* newspaper, Betty Dodson said that she does not believe that girls/women today are as sexually liberated as they think they are. She is re-launching her masturbation classes.

It was 1973 and a couple who were my close friends were "in love" for some twenty years. The wife died, leaving the husband heartbroken. Other friends and I did our best to comfort him. Eventually we encouraged him to start socializing. After two years of searching, he met a divorced woman who he felt could fill the void he was experiencing. He knew that I was working on my counseling degree and confided in me. This woman he met was loving, caring and they shared interests. The problem was that she had never experienced an orgasm. She was afraid to approach sex for fear of failure. I told my friend about Masters and Johnson's *Human Sexual Response* and their findings on clitoral orgasm. He read the book and asked if I could guide him to ascertain appropriate time periods for each step. He wanted to help the woman he loved share the delight of a sexual union with him. I agreed to guide him.

He started his approach by showing his caring in an unthreatening and non-sexual manner. First, when lying on the carpet in front of her fireplace, or attending a play or movie, he would avoid physical touching. Each phase lasted a week. The next step was gently touching her hand. In time, she felt more secure and he attempted more intimate touching. It took more than two months for her to joyfully climax with cunnilingus. She felt safe enough to allow him to climax with intercourse. Their love bonding became deeper when they were finally able to overcome their obstacles.

In 1975, psychologist Lonnie Garfield Barbach, PhD wrote *For Yourself: The Fulfillment of Female Sexuality*. It presents a realistic guideline for females to take the time, to know, enjoy and assume responsibility for their sexuality and liberate other aspects of their lives. They became more comfortable with their bodies and self-worth. It became easier to communicate sexual intimacies as well as non-sexual needs to a partner. A greater self-assurance spread into social areas of their lives. Guides are available in Lonnie Garfield Barbach's book. You will find specific approaches for making the time, finding an appropriate place and an open attitude for learning to achieve personal sexual pleasures.

"Angelica" was a client who compared masturbation to opening Pandora's Box. She tried to overcome fear of the unknown and allowing herself the freedom to explore deep sexual emotions. She did not know what it would lead to or if she could cope with it. Achieving orgasm by accepting responsibility for her own sexuality was exciting. She began to feel safe, because she could now trust her own body. It helped her overcome other social fears with relationships and work.

One client, "Matthew," related his experiences with early masturbation. He described it as a new physical and emotional sensation that felt good. He enjoyed it whenever circumstances and privacy would allow. Boys begin masturbation at a younger age and the repetition is more frequent than it is in girls. The penis is easily viewed, stimulated by clothing, bathing, touching and urinating. Erections are not always controllable during the "raging hormone age."

Available information about this new sexual freedom was helpful for me. I was divorced from 1973 to 2001 and I was not always with an ongoing sexual partner. During this period, I was teaching full time, experiencing financial stress and was caring for an adult daughter with medical problems. It was no surprise that I found it difficult to climax over a period, with or without a partner. I learned to relax, and I enjoyed concentrating on my sexual needs when I was alone. I was no longer anxious about needing a partner. In time, I experienced that same emotionality with a partner. It certainly relieved stress and created relaxation and indescribable pleasure.

With the advent of the Women's Liberation Movement, there were men who were confused about new social rules regarding opening doors for women and who pays the check for dinner. Some men were angry with the changes in women's self-determination in the workplace, the bedroom and when to procreate. But there were those men who accepted women's changing status with grace.

Inspired by the Women's Liberation Movement, Sam Julty and other leaders of the Men's Liberation Movement helped to clarify men's self-identity and their social roles in the early 1970s. This freed some men from feeling obligated to devote themselves only to financial caring for the family. They made attempts to understand who they were and learned how to discover and utilize their creative interests. Some of these men could now show more love to their families. Others left the family unit to find their identity and how they fit into new social values. Sam Julty wrote *Male Sexual Performance*, *Men's Bodies, Men's Selves* and *IMPOTENCE: Malady and Myth*.

I met Sam Julty in 1973. He helped me understand and become more compassionate towards the realities of men's issues. I appreciated his frankness. Sam told me that men are apprehensive about being accepted when calling a woman for a "date." He expected me to call him as well and to please be prompt for dates. Sam said that he worked just as hard as I did to earn money, so we should each pay for our own expenses. I thought that was fair reasoning.

During that time, men benefited from women's courageous battles for personal freedom. A society that frees one frees all. When one is imprisoned all are imprisoned.

In 1974, I met someone who helped me understand that sexual incapacities can be overcome with caring responses for achieving mutual pleasures. It was interesting for me to be with a man who could bring me to climax and reach his own intense and pleasurable climax, without attaining an erection.

In the early 1950s, I was a receptionist at the Workshop School of Commercial Art, in the 666 Fifth Avenue freight elevator building, around the corner from the Museum of Modern Art. My responsibility was recording the comings and goings of famous artists who taught classes and the models who posed. In the middle of a cold winter, "Jonas" entered the office without a winter coat. He had been living in Paris and told our director Milt Wynne that he was destitute. Milt knew of this artist and arranged for him to teach a class. I saw Jonas regularly during my two years at the Workshop.

In 1977, I was teaching 1st and 2nd grade students and read a *Scholastic* newsletter to the class. In it, was an article about Jonas who was now a famous illustrator of children's books. His books were the first I knew of that depicted realistic African American families with affection. The children loved the vibrant colors on each page and the cute little stories.

I was happy to read about Jonas' success and I wrote to him through the *Scholastic* newsletter. He remembered me and called to find out if I was single. Jonas was traveling extensively at that time. It was a year until his itinerary slowed down enough for us to have lunch and dinners for a time.

Jonas had a prostate problem. Intercourse was painful, so we spent a lovely night together abstaining from it. This was most endearing, with Jonas holding and touching me affectionately all night long. I had a delightful experience with a man who could not have sexual intercourse.

In 1982 Jonas stopped calling and didn't answer his phone. I was worried and went to his Manhattan apartment. He looked grim. I told him that his silence concerned me and I asked why hadn't I heard from him. Jonas told me his prostate condition was cancerous and terminal. He asked me not to be offended, but he didn't want to see anyone. He died in 1983.

On June 1, 2013, Bruce to Caitlin Jenner announced her changing sexuality. This made me recall someone, who in the late eighties, died because he did not have the freedom to publicly express his crossdressing self. "Barton" was a construction worker in my community who had known me as a teacher. He heard that I retired and was a practicing therapist. He scheduled a therapeutic appointment with me. Barton had a gruff kind of personality and appearance. He was in a good functioning marriage. They had children and adopted others because Barton had been an orphan. He told me that he was always a crossdresser. His wife accepted that prior to having children. Afterwards, she insisted that it become secret to avoid social ridicule the children might have to deal with.

In the early days of their marriage his wife accompanied him to public places on occasion, when he dressed as a woman. As time passed, she didn't want to do that anymore. Barton started to experience chest infections that only the feel of feminine clothing against his skin could alleviate. He kept his feminine clothing in a secret place to wear when alone at home. I agreed that he could wear feminine clothes to our therapy sessions. Barton looked awkward in women's clothing. He was not attractive when he wore huge crinoline slips under his skirt, high heels he could hardly master and makeup that didn't cover his beard.

Barton told me that he appreciated being able to talk to someone he trusted and that would keep this information confidential. He reminded me how important it was to control his chest infections by feeling feminine attire against his skin. In time, he pleaded with me for a therapeutic session in which I would accompany him to a public place dressed as a woman. I didn't feel up to going to a restaurant, with him looking as unpleasant as he did. I optioned for a park where I race-walked. Barton agreed and wobbled along in his high heels behind me. People gasped at the sight of him. It didn't matter anymore, because I helped fulfill his need.

This man eventually discontinued therapy. Some years later, his son called to tell me that his father was in the hospital and wanted to see me. He was near death with a lung infection. He asked to see me alone and almost apologetically told me that he not been able to cross-dress to control his infection. He thanked me for my kindness and died days after I saw him. So much for our punishing cultural judgements of other sexual or dress differences. In 2016, this had been challenged and has become acceptable to a sizeable degree.

Caitlin's public "coming out" statement said this was a way to help young people feel comfortable with their sexual individuality, as well as for her own freedom. Currently, some in their "twelve through twenties" are making their own sexual and social rules by demonstrating their values opposing inhumane economics, war and racism issues.

In the 1960s and 1970s young people of various sexual orientations attempted to experience a universal and non-judgmental era of peace, love and sex. At "love-ins" during the opposition to the Vietnam War, the impassioned chant was to "make love not war." Demonstrations were numerous. From 2015, prominent protest movements like Occupy Now, Black Lives Matter and individual local groups are prevalent once again. The aspiration is to create a more compassionate world.

There are young people who use drugs as a means of coping with their distrust and anger towards elders who control society. That rebelliousness extends to sexuality. Females dress and speak quite provocatively to entice males. Young males freely verbalize sexual desires. That paradigm exists in the gay and lesbian communities as well. A mutual understanding seems to prevail that sex is available with the first "hello" and even before that "hello."

From 1949 on, I knew people who functioned in the sub cultures of mainstream society. They were bohemians, gays, lesbians, artists, actors and musicians whose sexual decisions were unique. Then, in the 1960s, my grown children told me about the peace and love era and the new sexual freedom. I heard the Doors' song "*Hello, I Love You*" on television and it interested me. Parents were now listening to music that reflected the immediate sexual gratification their children were involved in. After the initial shock, a parent could offer protective information. No matter the time period or label, the issue is to avoid social diseases, unwanted pregnancies and emotional turmoil. It is still important to become more aware of your partner before intimacy.

The media's focus is purposefully developed to stimulate interests in music, clothes, sex and relationship attitudes that increase profit for corporations and disregard the welfare of our young people. There are teenagers who have declared cultural independence with strong ties and total absorption with the Internet. Despite the dominance of social media, it is important for young adults in our culture to find guidance for averting personal and social problems.

There is a general disconnect from parental guidance. However, parental approval is usually required for the birth control pill. This becomes problematic when those who are sexually active are trying to avoid unplanned or unwanted pregnancies. Oral and anal sex are engaged in, at times to prevent pregnancy. Some males and females request the use of a condom because they are concerned about disease and pregnancy. It is important to observe and question the cleanliness and sexual habits of someone with whom one desires to have sex. An article in the Westchester/Rockland edition of *The Journal News*, dated October 4, 2011, discusses the HPV virus becoming more prevalent orally in both men and women due to the increase of oral sex. When there is a lack of parental involvement, there is also a lack of awareness about their children's sexual practices. As a result, no appropriate information is offered to prevent disease and unwanted pregnancies. Some parents with specific religious beliefs are opposed to their children receiving sexual information and access to birth control items.

In 2017, sexual practices still expected or demanded by some are used to attract and maintain a momentary or longer relationship. The "my girl" phenomenon is the assumption that the female should belong to a male and females believe that they must be attached to a male to be accepted. One would think that the concepts of the women's liberation movement of the 1970s would have filtered down to our present generation of young women through their grandmothers and mothers.

Sex can be an intensely pleasurable physical experience, especially during the teen years and into the twenties. "Mother Nature" planned it that way to ensure the continuation of the human species. That sexual intensity is the "raging hormone" experience young people cope with, along with stressful competition and the fear of not being chosen. The combined stresses of strong sexual urges with a need for peer group status, can create intense emotions and a tolerance for cruel sexual experiences. Adult guidance that can help thwart problematic personal and social situations is a prime prerequisite not always utilized.

Teenagers having babies are generally unequipped emotionally and financially to bring the newborn into a stable family life. It complicates the child's concept of future relationships and social involvements. That premature responsibility of the young raising the young robs the teenager of their own youth and the future they could be preparing for. Adults are especially responsible for providing sexual education that offers birth control information and helps young people to understand feelings about the sexual desires they are experiencing. Pleasuring oneself enables young people to relieve anxiety and enjoy their sexual sensations. According to Lonnie Garfield Barbach, PhD in *For Yourself: The Fulfillment of Female Sexuality*, one of the best ways to learn about your sexual responses and consequently enable you to teach your partner how to stimulate your sexual pleasure and orgasm, is by pleasuring oneself.

Teenage sexual energy can also become somewhat sublimated with sports, or creative, intellectual and spiritual endeavors. Individualized education for goal development and achievement fosters a feeling of self-accomplishment, pride and self-worth. This can influence how and who one chooses for companionable and sexual relationships.

Sexual, emotional and physical childhood trauma and a culture controlled by media have their effects on our teenage population. A client, "Terese" reenacting her childhood trauma, by choosing a man who would leave for various reasons, just like her father did. "Beth" recycled a terrorizing childhood trauma, choosing men who could cause her to be frightened in some way. These young women learned how to use the effects of childhood trauma recycling to make the transition from living through unpleasant past experiences and journeying into the living reality of the present moment. They became attracted to males who they described as "nice people" and with whom they feel much less stress. They began to feel safer and more confident in asking questions which could reveal the kind of persons they are interacting with. They can express their own needs in the process of developing compassionate relationships with the Journey to Now.

Robert Sorensen in *Adolescent Sexuality in Contemporary America* writes that interviews indicate how young people view their sexuality. The physical pleasure includes getting along with the opposite sex, not hurting others and being wanted. It involves belonging to someone who understands and can exchange common thoughts. Sex for young people can be a means of communication, conforming with a peer group, challenging parents and society, escaping loneliness and other adolescent pressures.

The feeling of doing something "bad" because I was having pre-marital sex in 1944 doesn't have to be experienced with correct sex education for the young in 2017. Factual parental guidance for sex information begins with the naming of the rectum, penis, vagina or breasts, along with toilet training. Responding to questions about body functions and sex should be brief and to the point. Information about private body parts and creating boundaries for who can or who is not permitted to touch them is a concept even a young child can understand. This includes telling someone if the boundaries are crossed. *How to Talk with Teens about Love, Relationships, and Sex: A Guide for Parents* by Amy G. Miron, M. S. and Charles D. Miron, PhD is a perfect book for parents who feel uncomfortable or not equipped to discuss sex with their children. It has excellent conversation starters and "just the facts' information. *Uncommon Sense for Parents with Teenagers* by Michael Riera, PhD addresses parenting, understanding and discussing sexuality with teenagers.

With the *Journey to Now* experience, parents can set an example wherein young people can learn the concept of living in the here and NOW, rather than recycling childhood traumas into current relationships. Youthful and exuberant energies can be utilized for the beauty of choosing relationships of any sexual orientation, based on self-respect, self-pride, companionship and the joy of sharing love.

In 2017, we are in an era of constant and unstable shifts in economics, politics and weather. The advent of immediate information isn't always correct, and contradictions can be distressing. The converse is to challenge this culture and stimulate our conscious efforts to become a catalyst. We need to create constructive education, economic freedoms and personal expression for ourselves and the oncoming generation. My protocol guides your ability to see people and incidents more clearly and rapidly for making better decisions.

When I was modeling, a friend who was going off to World War II, asked for my picture.

CHAPTER 16

We Can Enjoy Senior Sex

Old Woman versus Mature Man

She's a sloppy dresser but his clothes are casual
She's letting herself go but he has a little paunch
She's a wrinkled old bag but he has charming lifelines
She has a new boy toy but look at his new young chick
Young chicks turn him on but her young men get sex lessons
Shouldn't judging looks and mores be the same for each sex?
Artists, musicians, sculptors, poets, philosophers
Feeling joy, sensing those momentary conceptions
Create beauty from instantaneous reactions
With love, respect for wisdom that all ages offer,
Beauty in those female wrinkles, and lowered breasts can
Indicate years of learned lessons and passion to share
Not negative judgments that discard mature women.

We adjust our activities as changes occur with the passage of time. Skateboarding is exciting at fourteen. Dancing, race-walking are buoyant pursuits at sixty plus, can sustain joy from using other skills you developed. The intense sexual energy rush you remember from your youth and expect with senior sex could lead to disappointment, hurt, or anger. "Mature" sex offers an exquisitely deeper combination of emotional and physical reactions. At age sixty plus, you are a sexagenarian, so let's explore!

On September 7, 2016, the 60-year-old actress, comedienne, producer and talk show host Whoopi Goldberg appeared on Stephen Colbert's Late Show. They discussed her anti-relationship book *If Someone Says "You Complete Me," RUN!* Whoopi was asked about sexual relationships. Holding up her hands she said that these hands know where everything is. They know where to go when they are needed. Whoopi said that she is not willing to do the hard work required in relationships. But there is nothing wrong with a good friend, every so often, who knows how to hit the right spot.

Bernard D. Starr, PhD and Macello Baker Weiner, E.D.D.'s book *Sex and Sexuality in the Mature Years* presents questions asked of seniors about what sex means to them now in their lives. The answers were that sex makes older people feel beautiful, desirable, exhilarated and young. They considered sex to be a most important part of a relationship.

In response to questions about sexual activity, senior citizens declared frequency to be once or twice a week. A minority of respondents reported a decline in sexual response and feelings. This was especially true for men who described erection problems. One man in his forties, despite having an erection problem, was still able to please his sexual partner with affection, caring, stimulating touching and oral sex. After bringing his partner to climax, he climaxed loudly and gleefully.

Despite this man's inability to attain an erection, his inner sexual energies enabled him to provide sexual pleasure for his partner and himself. Kirlian photography would have indicated his sexual desires. It captures a multi colored aura that extends from our inner being to our outer environment. Kirlian photography reflects and depicts the energy or "life force" that every living being possesses. The varied colors in the aura indicate where the body's concentration of inner emotional and physical states of energy are located. That inner energy field is shown in the aura surrounding the outside of the body. This markedly illustrates how our inner energies can affect our outer environment. The *Journey to Now* focuses on the physical reaction that accompanies the inner energy of emotional trauma. The recognition of that physical reaction is used to guide our social choices of behavior.

The Human Aura, Astral Colors and Thought Forms, by Swami Panchadasi describes the human aura as a fine ethereal radiation or emanation surrounding every living human being; the magnetic atmosphere that can extend from two to three feet in all directions from the body.

My own sexuality varied from the intensity of a teenager to the beauty of young adulthood experiences. In my early twenties and later in my forties, I found it difficult to climax due to intense stressful conflict during those times in my life. In my mid-forties, I was relaxed and feeling comfortable with my self-identity and with sex. Climaxing was very pleasurable. Currently, at ninety years of age, sex is delightful and intense. My husband is an exhilarating sexual partner. The deep connection is due to trust, a safe feeling and an anticipatory desire to satisfy each other. Intense climaxes continue to surprise me. Physical problems or daily stress can affect sexual desire. Don't be discouraged. It can always get better when you clarify and focus your inner being with this protocol. So, enjoy love, life and sex.

Love can be experienced more than once in a lifetime. Life changes and adjusts with time, experiences and circumstances. Our needs and attractions vary. The anthropologist Margaret Mead wrote *Coming of Age in Samoa* in 1928 and continued her work through the 1970s. She commented on the need for different partners at various stages in our lives. There could be a partner for the more carefree young adulthood period, another for the time to bear children and raise them and one for empty nesters who now have the freedom to explore the world. One relationship that can modify through it all, satisfy each other's needs and create deep love is a fortunate one. It can also be surprising and exciting to find love at one or more phases of a lifetime.

Two Equals One

Skin to skin, no separation
Touch and hold, no preparation

131

Your brown stomach and body hair
My breasts touching you everywhere
We exchange warmth that pierces through
We are one, my me and your you.
Serenity in our touching
An openness without clutching
Our body aromas inhaled
With an ecstasy we exhaled
Our loving tongues that caress
All love exchanges without stress,
Skin to skin, no separation
Touch and hold, no preparation.

Various advertisements for products in lifestyle catalogues, such as those magazines for active healthy living, the disabled, senior products and household items, display offers for sexual enhancers as Magic Messengers or Butterfly Kisses Massagers, ring systems (to maintain erections) and pills for "fast and safe" erections. There are DVD's illustrating intense sex for men and women under and over fifty. Eve's Garden's office in Manhattan is a valuable resource for guidance and the exploration of sex toys. They can be reached at www.evesgarden.com. There is an apparent desire for these products and there are similar centers in most cities throughout the world.

In 2017, it is generally acknowledged that people over fifty, sixty, seventy and eighty still get aroused. They want to enjoy all the sexual pleasure there is for them to experience. An advantage is that pregnancy is no longer a concern in most cases. The freedom from children who are grown and living with their own families, are no longer a daily disruption. The senior in the last stages of life realizes that time is shorter for pleasurable explorations than in any other period of their lives. There are seniors who retreat into sadness when they could journey into the realm of NOW. Benefits for the emotional, physical, creative and sexual areas of senior lives correlates with the effort to experience the *Journey to Now.*

Being with someone who cares about your welfare is certainly gratifying, especially if you are disabled. There is a difference between being alone and being lonely. It is a good choice to be alone rather than with someone who is abusive, emotionally and/or physically. Lonely, at a senior age can be the result of being abandoned by family, feeling helpless because of a physical disability, or for other reasons. Participating in senior center activities can stimulate your interests. Volunteering to help someone else can make your life more purposeful and enjoyable. Experiencing this protocol can promote the concept of living the true you. You can develop more accurate judgment for beneficial companionship with someone who could be in your life. A situation that is not entirely what one would wish for can be improved with the use of the protocol.

It is ideal when one can feel safe with someone who can be trusted. A person who you can feel affection for, share daily body massages with and pre-sexual or sexual body intimacy. Learning to allow self-love for pleasuring oneself can be a surprisingly joyful experience. Using hands, sex toys, romantic music and/or visualization could enhance solo or sexual experiences with a partner. Self-pleasuring allows us to identify sexual needs. This can be communicated to a partner when sharing an intimate experience.

Sex at any age is pleasurably stimulating. It wakes up the hormones affecting our emotional, physical and spiritual being. One should check with your medical advisor before venturing into this joyful world of sexual loving. Diet, exercise, meditation, chanting, praying, effects our sexual functioning. Dr. Gary Null's DVD *Sexual Healing*, demonstrates relaxed, caring and informative suggestions for sharing love, even if the sharing is with yourself.

CHAPTER 17

Don't Retire Your Wisdom and Skills

In 2010, my adult daughter underwent two heart surgeries and was hospitalized for over three months. Her prognosis was a minute to minute death watch. I traveled to her hospital every day. I chanted consistently for her, I chanted with her, to change her energy path. She survived and recuperated at home. The experience I shared with her felt as though I was walking alongside her, through her "valley of death." It made me realize that eighty-four years of age was much closer to death than my earlier years. My daughter's rehabilitation allowed me to think about what was I going to do during the next twenty years of my life. I was determined to complete *From Birth to Death with Sex In Between*. I had not been working on it consistently since 2008 because of other responsibilities. The knowledge I have accumulated and presented in this book can help anyone live more joyful lives. The *Don't Retire Your Wisdom and Skills* chapter is a gift for seniors. I'm looking forward to another project of interest after the publication of this book.

At age fifteen, youthful concerns may be oriented towards excelling in sports, having the right hair style or clothes and being accepted by peers. Teenagers who develop their talents in music, art, writing, dance, building things, math, science and/or sports can be stimulated by those experiences. Specialized training can help them focus on specific goals. Guidance from elders can show them ways to achieve those goals by modeling their elders, constructive discussions and consistent efforts.

Time passes and at the age of eighteen, colleges, trade schools, or work become immediate considerations. Those who are more fortunate can train for and/or work at what they have the aptitude for. Some struggle to find out who they are, others focus on achieving financial independence. Conditions exists where there are inadequate education or work opportunities. There can be the additional personal burden of family financial instability. The resulting frustration can be directed towards destructive ways of obtaining money immediately.

At age thirty, one may or may not have a family to support, but may be studying to further one's goals, or working to fulfill personal financial obligations. The fortunate ones can become financially self- sustaining because of educational pursuits, hobbies and/or talent. Others can only use available free time to pursue their special interests. When there is disinterest in daily work routines that are necessary for sustaining lifestyles or obligations, energies may be diverted to destructive pastimes.

How do you adjust from your fifties to your nineties? Eight hours of work might not be filling the day? Will you watch television to fill those eight hours? Is a solution volunteering for some special cause you always felt a compassion for? Rodney Brooks' October 22, 2014 article in *USA Today* entitled *"6 networking tips for retirees,"* suggests creating a business card indicating that you are a retired business owner, plumber or electrician offering counseling. Call five friends a day and talk with each of them for ten minutes. Websites like AARP and LinkedIn can help you maintain contact in your fields of expertise with meetings you can attend. You have time for free non-credit courses at local community colleges. Reading events at bookstores and libraries are a good place to sit and read. The more you keep your mind active, the more you prevent Alzheimer's.

DON'T RETIRE. You have wisdom and a lifetime of skills to share. Your special knowledge could benefit many younger people. Creativity, work experience and education are treasures a mature person can share with youth. Exchange your valuable information with others by offering your specialties where they are needed. This can be done through work- shops, libraries and other organizations. Money management, research, art, music, dance, relationships and your other achievements can help others and may provide extra income for you and can become a fulfilling experience. On September 14, 2014 Susan Ricker wrote an article in *The Journal News' Career Builder* section entitled *"Rewarding Vocations for Retirees."* She states that retirees can utilize previous work experience, but with less intense schedules. One can accept leadership positions for mentoring that are based on accumulated professional knowledge. Dance or crafts instructor, dog walker, driver, care giver to the elderly, financial advisor, freelance editor or writer, garden store employee, house watcher and retail store salesperson are suggested. These are choices for an extra paycheck or doing a good deed, or creating a change of pace.

The senior years do come. A lack of satisfying productivity can be depressing and affect us emotionally and physically. Contemplate planning the latter part of your life with the realization that you're closer to death than your birth. How would you want to spend the rest of your life? Make your remaining years productive and enjoyable. If you didn't have the opportunity to find your true inner being in your youth, express it NOW. It's not too late to begin the *Journey to Now* that can guide the transformation of fear and anxiety into serenity. Energies that were consumed by depression, anger, or other painful emotions can be converted and utilized to create a more satisfying life structure. The education or reeducation at high school adult classes, colleges or workshops can prepare you for new or improved ventures. Diet and exercise at all levels, can result in a better functioning mind and body for a sustainable future life. Dr. Gary Null's DVD entitled *Seven Steps to Perfect Health*, can provide valuable information to that effect.

You can learn to overcome the apprehension of social conflicts with *Journey to Now* as your guide for living with more tranquility. The energy of our joyous outlook is transmitted to others. Inspiring and compassionate social behavior can be a pleasurable experience for you. That is a key for creating a more concerned and humane community. This is the kind of caring world I want to live in. So, I was moved when I heard Michael Jackson's heartfelt plea for that to happen in *"Heal The World"*. His song was inspiring for me, for the young and old who loved Michael's performances to make this planet Earth a better place for everyone.

CHAPTER 18

My Family's Pet Caring

When I was seven years old my brother brought home a Police dog puppy. It was my responsibility to feed her and take her out during the day. I was told she came onto my bed when I was asleep and stayed with me every night. Queenie became my pet. I would take her outside with me while I played with friends. I didn't have to put a leash on Queenie because she never left my side. One cold winter morning at 6:00 AM my father let Queenie out as usual in what was a rural Bronx neighborhood in New York City. This time she didn't come back. We called and searched for her but we could not find Queenie. I was heartbroken.

In my mid-twenties, I was living on eight acres surrounded by woods in a very rural area of Rockland County, New York. We had chickens and geese. The geese would nip at my three-year-old daughter's rear end as she tried to walk away. Our chickens were fed natural foods and ate the grass that surrounded our one-acre organic garden. Their eggs were deep yellow and had a rich, delicious taste. Someone gave me a cat with whom I developed a loving relationship for about two years. Our sparsely peopled area seemed to be safe for her to be an inside/outside cat. One day we found her on the road in front of our house. She was hit by one of the two cars that traveled our road each day. It was heartbreaking for me.

In my later twenties, I was still living in that same rural area. We were given a collie puppy. Mo was never leashed and never left the property. My daughter at that time was a two-year-old unsteady walker. Lyn would hold on to Mo's body for support and he never moved away from her while she needed assistance. At about the same time someone gave us

Tangee, a beautiful ring-tailed monkey. She would help herself to bananas she peeled and nuts she would crack open. There was always a trail of skins and shells wherever she went. Years later, we picked a beagle. He fought battles with clothes that were drying on an outdoor line and barked at a neighbor's mop that was put out to dry.

More time passed and we chose a bright, active wire-haired fox terrier puppy. Terry sat in front of the kitchen sink, looked upwards and made the sound Wa-Wa. It was more subdued and different than barking. He was asking for water from the sink and we gave it to him. He preferred drinking that instead of the water that was already in his dish. Terry would also go to the back door through which he was usually taken out. He made a similar sound as when asking for water. This time it was Ot-Ot not Wa-Wa. We could not allow him out without a leash because he would decide to run off for an adventure. He moved quickly when he found the opportunity to dash out from in between or around our legs. When we called him to come back home he would sit looking and listening from a slight distance. He was contemplating whether to run and he always ran. If you tried to approach him or raised your voice in anger he would head to his girlfriend's house nearby. To bring him back home I would drive to wherever he was, open the car door and say, "Terry, do you want a ride?" and he would jump into the car.

One day he escaped to a house a quarter of a mile from ours. There, someone had both a female dog in heat and a male dog in an eight-foot-high chain link enclosure. Terry scaled that fence, mated with the female dog and humped the male. The owner of those dogs called the police who called us to come and get Terry, who had already climbed out of the enclosure. I drove to where I was told he was. The scene I encountered was that of four policemen encircling Terry trying to catch him, but he was too fast for them. I opened my car door and simply said, "Terry, do you want a ride?" Terry jumped into my car and we headed home.

The owner of the dogs Terry visited took us to court. He accused Terry of raping his female dog and of the horror of having sex with the male. The owner yelled that his male dog would never try to have sex with the female and that Terry raped her. While he was yelling, the elderly owner's adult daughter stood next to him, head bent and sobbing loudly. The judge fined me $25.00 for Terry's crimes. With an uncontrollable giggle, I said, "Are you kidding?" The judge, unsmiling replied, "One more word out of you and I'll double the fine."

My daughter and I bathed Terry and we loved cuddling with him. My son Lee, Lyn and I improvised complex games with Terry that he understood and responded to. It was always an adventure to take Terry with us when we ran errands. In his mind, he was the family protector. At an outdoor food market, someone arrived in a horse and carriage and placed it alongside the cars. I parked next to that horse and carriage and took Terry out of the car with me. Terry charged the horse to protect me from this large creature. It was all I could do to hold him back. At another time in New York City, Terry had to be held back from charging at a mastiff dog he thought was a threat to my daughter.

In my early forties, I became "single" again and was teaching grade school. I knew my homecoming times would be erratic so I didn't acquire any more pets to care for. Lyn took the pet baton from me. I gave her an interesting Abyssinian cat, Nikki, to care for in her own apartment. Lyn would sing "hello" to him in response to his meowing as she unlocked the apartment door. Nikki learned "hello" and replied back. Lyn trained this cat to react properly to several specific directions. He greeted those people he liked, but he did not like one of Lyn's boyfriends and growled at him. There were a few occasions when Lyn, who was diabetic, was experiencing serious insulin reactions while asleep. Once, Nikki, who was sleeping in another room, ran into the bedroom, jumped on top of Lyn, smacked her in the face and meowed loudly until she was cognitive. On another occasion, when Nikki couldn't wake Lyn, he moved on to her husband, smacked him until he woke up to help Lyn. The response to Lyn's love and caring for her pets was the love, devotion and protection they gave her. Eventually she lived in a house with a yard and gradually acquired four dogs and four cats.

Gabe (Gabriel), part Doberman and Rottweiler, was Lyn's first pet in her new house. He measured five feet tall when he stood up to kiss your face hello. He was a loving dog. Gabe was big enough to sit next to you on the couch with his rear feet touching the floor and his rear end sitting on the couch. He just wanted you to hold him and pet him. Lyn's mailman said that she didn't need an alarm system. Gabe's bark was loud and deep, and no one would come into the house unannounced. There were times when Lyn was ill, and it was hard for her to get up from the couch. Lyn would say, "We're going to bed." Gabe would position himself in front of her, enabling her to hold onto him so she could stand up. Gabe walked slowly at her side so that she could hold onto him as he accompanied her. The mutual devotion was strong and total.

Lyn had a very close relationship with her pets. She became a licensed animal rescuer and rehabilitated several abused cats. While walking her dogs in a neighborhood park, Lyn saw a tiny, scraggly kitten under a parked car. Every day for a week she brought food for the kitten until it felt safe and allowed Lyn to pick her up. Before it could come home, the kitten was taken to a vet for an examination and cleaning. At first Lyn would lay down on the carpet at a distance from where Daisy was lying. It took weeks before she could get close enough to pet her. Daisy was afraid of people and would only eat in a secluded area. That scrawny kitten grew up to be a beautiful, grey and white, thick-furred cat. Only Lyn could touch her, pick her up and cuddle her. In the evening, Daisy would come to Lyn to snuggle with her when she was sitting and reading but only after the dogs were asleep.

Lyn wanted to learn as much as she could to make her pets more comfortable, especially when they needed help. She wanted to make them happy. Dr. Micheal Fox's *Massage for Cats and Dogs* includes therapeutic and diagnostic massage that effects bonding. This helped Lyn to understand her pets' body language.

Lyn's dream was to develop a sanctuary for abused animals. She did that on a small scale inside her home and within a large enclosed lawn. Her dream was inspired by the book *Best Friends The True Story of the World's Most Beloved Animal Sanctuary* by Samantha Glen. It tells us about a

No Kill, world renowned sanctuary in Angel Canyon, in Kenal, Utah, that rescues pets and farm animals. Cabins are available for pet owners to stay (and volunteer) while their pets are being rehabilitated

In 2013 Lyn adopted an eleven-year-old poodle that no one else wanted. He had cancer, among other problems and his right hind leg didn't function. Because of Lyn's loving care, Sammy's cancer stabilized, and his other problems improved. He waddled behind the other three dogs and barked loudly to let Lyn know when he was hungry, needed to be let out, or to be picked up. Sammy's physical condition reflected the abuse he experienced in the past, but he lived in the NOW. He made sure he let people know what his immediate needs were. Lyn lived in the NOW along with Sammy. Lyn, who was disabled by her illnesses, developed a rewarding daily routine. She accomplished chores and enjoyed recreation and relaxation for herself as well as for her beloved pets.

Cesar's Way The Natural Everyday Guide to Understanding and Correcting Common Dog Problems is by the world renowned Dog Whisperer, Cesar Millan, who writes about the role of the "pack-leader." Lyn applied Cesar's method and developed acceptable pet behavior. She taught her dogs and cats to respond when daily routine directions were given. This left time for the fun and affection they all enjoyed. Lyn fulfilled her pets' needs and her own.

Dr. Gary Null's book and DVD *Natural Pet Care* helped Lyn understand how she could improve her pets' quality of life with diet, exercise, bathing, grooming and understanding animal behavior. Lyn showed a special love for her pets by utilizing an alternative approach that benefited them.

People have pets for companionship, personal protection, as service dogs to compensate for disabilities, or just because they love them.

Lyn once told me she trusted animals more than she trusted people. I understood what she meant because it was her pets who never failed to give back the kindness they received from her. Those of us who were hurt by the way adults treated us can benefit from the *Journey to Now* process. It can help to rapidly identify persons we should avoid and to recognize those we can trust. Becoming self-protective, choosing relationships that are congenial produces less conflict, stress and anger. The awareness of and functioning in accord with our true needs helps us feel harmonious and able to express ourselves more humanely.

Our socially interactive behavior which includes one's pets is usually expressed by recycling old traumas. You can live your true being in the HERE and NOW by recognizing the "old stuff" and working productively with it through the protocol. As night follows day, the way you relate to your pets is a continuum of the kind of relationship you have with yourself and the world around you.

Our families' attitude towards our pets was an ever-flowing stream that collected and carried our love and caring for them.

NIKKI rescued Lyn from insulin reactions and liked saying "hello" to Lyn when she came home from work.

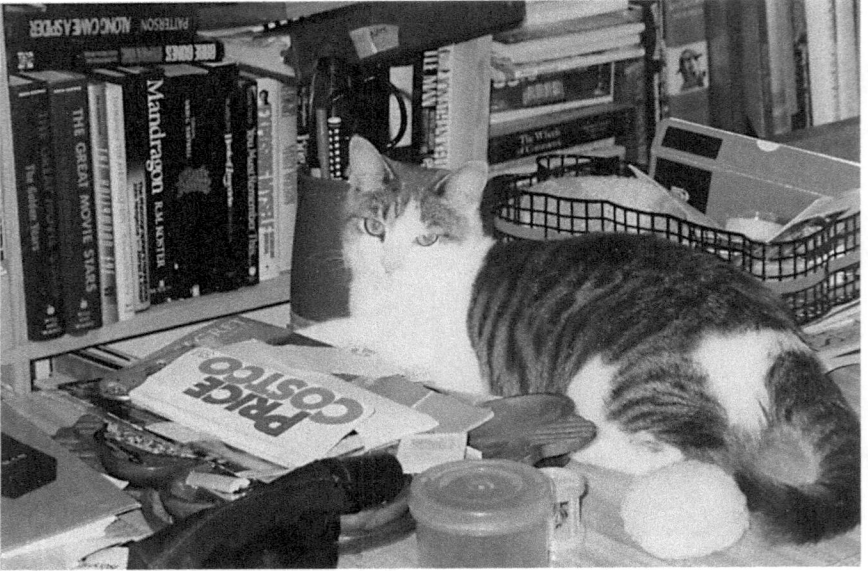

DAISY was the abused and emaciated cat that Lyn rescued.

GABE was a loving companion and he helped Lyn walk.

GABE and LYN enjoyed each other's company.

ANNIE was very devoted to Lyn and protected her and the new puppy Tyler.

CHAPTER 19

Coping with the Loss of a Loved One

Lyn at 15.

At eighty-nine, I revisited the "death issue." I had already experienced the death of my mother, father, sister, two brothers and others I was close to. I coped with each loss differently, depending upon my relationship with the departed and my life situation at that time.

In 1956, I was twenty-nine and in a marriage with an emotionally cruel person. My mother was at death's door for seven years. Her weight eventually went down to sixty pounds and she passed away from stomach cancer. I visited her every weekend and those long seven years eventually became non-traumatic. Our relationship had been strained since I was eleven years old and I felt concern but little or no emotion for her as I got older. When she died, I felt a vague emptiness in a space where something I couldn't name had been. As the years passed I realized my mother lived her life as a victim and I can feel compassion for her.

My father died in 1975. I was forty-seven, newly divorced, teaching 1st and 2nd grade. I earned a B.A. degree and was working on my Counseling Master's program. I loved my father unconditionally as a young child. Into adulthood I loved him despite his foibles. At forty-six I was disappointed when I realized my father was not wise enough to understand that I was the only one of his children who was not interested in his money and was truly devoted to him. I no longer felt emotionally attached to him, but I continued to show the respect due to my father. I understood that he had not been in a happy relationship with my mother, yet never neglected his financial responsibility for the family. When he died, I flew to Florida for his funeral. Immediately upon landing I was driven to a funeral parlor. I was led into a small room and instantly faced an open coffin with my father's face confronting me. I was shocked and became hysterical. I felt as though a root was pulled out from right under me. I was then ushered into a room where cousins, aunts and uncles I hadn't seen for forty years hugged and kissed me. It was like a wedding reception. They remembered me as the child in my family who was sociable and affectionate. Their heartwarming greetings made me feel loved. When I arrived back home my father's passing left me with a strange, sad emptiness. I could no longer call him every Saturday to say hello and see how he was doing.

I was fifty years old when my brother Sam called to tell me my brother Ruby's wife died. Everyone in the family had a troubled relationship with Ruby. Sam urged me to call him to express my sympathy because it was the proper thing to do. He did not know that Ruby abused me as a child. I called Ruby to please Sam. Ruby asked me where I was in my life at that moment. I told him that I was divorced, working on my Master's and teaching young children. He said that I was the most intelligent one in the family. I felt a sudden constricting hurt in my throat because of my old conflict with him. It was painful to hear my brother compliment me. It magnified the childhood trauma he inflicted. I was not capable of speaking and could not ask him to explain the abuse. His praise was an insult. First, he hurt me and now, had the nerve to compliment me. It could not excuse his behavior.

When I was sixty years old with a Master's Degree in Counseling, Sam called to tell me that Ruby had died. I thought back to my last dis-cussion with Ruby. I recalled the unpleasant conflict and pain it caused me and my eyes became teary. I lived half my life recycling the trauma reactions of Ruby's abuse. Before I became a *Nichiren Shoshu Buddhist* and developed the *Journey to Now*, I chose men like him who could hurt me emotionally. The most damaging aspect of those choices were the consequences that affected my children.

I was eighty years old when my sister Sally died. Growing up we had an emotionally combative relationship. Until I was born Sally was the only pampered female child for six and a half years. I ruined her position in the family. I was always sick, needing my mother's care. Sally was neglected. She was jealous and angry because I was born. It wasn't until I was in my fifties, when she had moved to another state, that our relation-ship evolved into a "telephone camaraderie." I was sad that she developed Alzheimer's toward the end of her life. Sally's daughter Made-line and I developed a loving relationship during Sally's illness and passing. I am very grateful for this.

When I was eighty-five, my "kind brother" Sam, died. He was a good person, but not compassionately sensitive to others with value systems different from his. As a child, I was his "pet" in the family. The family teased me and told me that when Sam came home from college late at night, he kissed me goodnight while I was fast asleep. When I was a young child he made it known that he cared about my life. Sam made suggestions on my behalf that were immediately accepted by my family.

Sam was my role model for what a caring male should be. I was hurt and I cried when he married and moved to another state. I felt the loss of his daily presence and saw him only on special occasions. During my formative teen to adult years, Sam didn't make an effort to inquire or influence my parents about my future and the importance of my education. He was the only family member who could have influenced them to make the right decisions, because he was respected and admired. In my adult years, Sam rejected the choices I made in my life. I continued to call him with the change of seasons and visited him occasionally. I tried to show my appreciation for the love he gave me when I was young. I felt hurt when Sam died. I relived losing him for a second time. I ached and was conflicted. I knew he could've made such a difference in my life, had he cared enough. I experienced a difficult month before I could overcome the sorrow.

My daughter, Lyn, was born into an emotionally stormy marriage and she endured the consequences. Her health became compromised with diabetes in 1973. Throughout a thirty-year period, I was the only person who took care of Lyn's countless medical emergencies. I continued that effort for four years into her stressful 1993 marriage. My support of Lyn through her daily emotional and physical crises ended with her passing.

In 1999 Lyn was on the list for a kidney transplant. I knew that she would not make it to the year of 2000 if she didn't get one. I became depressed and found it difficult to function. I didn't know if I could survive her death. I was at a business meeting and I couldn't focus on the issues. The person in charge of the meeting knew of Lyn's situation. He raised his voice telling me not to allow the physical problems of others to enter my being. I was shocked, but I valued his opinion. I returned home and chanted *Nam-Myoho-Renge-Kyo*. It helped me understand how right this friend was. As a therapist, I helped clients with the loss of their loved ones. I encouraged them to review the Journey to Now. It could ease their pain by separating recycled trauma from reactions to the present situation. For those who were interested, I suggested *Nichiren Shoshu Buddhist* chanting for the deceased to transition to the very next existence with wonderful health and life karma. I supported the client's experiences when mourning and encouraged them to live the most beautiful life possible. I reminded them that their journey would honor their own lives and that of the deceased.

I followed my own advice. I realized I had been living Lyn's emotional life for her and I stopped. I did continue to be emotionally supportive when she related incidents from her stressful marriage and her continual health problems. I separated the loving compassion I had for her life from that of my own life force. I had to survive and avoid becoming a depleted caretaker who would not be able to help her. I related my daily adventures to Lyn because she had become socially isolated. It was a pleasing and stimulating window into a world she could become part of emotionally.

Dear One

The sun stopped shining
The rose stopped blooming
The wind stopped blowing
The birds stopped singing
The dogs stopped romping
Children stopped playing
My voice stopped laughing
My joy stopped beaming
My heart is aching
My child is dying
You can't be leaving
Dear one keep fighting.

Lyn died at the age of sixty after having endured about thirty surgeries since the age of eighteen. I no longer had to be cognizant of her physical and emotional suffering. It freed part of my guarded emotional pain. I knew that Lyn was not going to live to a grand old age, but I no longer had to wonder when that last day would come. Without that gnawing fear of her impending death I could better understand her life and our lives together. I chanted *Nam-Myoho-Renge-Kyo* and reviewed the *Journey to Now*. I cried with the profound realization that my daughter died. I missed Lyn's physical presence. My husband Manny was there for me with emotionally compassionate responses twenty-four hours a day. He helped to soothe my pain. We had a memorial service for Lyn at the *Nichiren Shoshu Buddhist Temple* in Flushing, New York, where she became a Buddhist in 1975. At the Temple, I was surrounded by loving and caring people who helped ease my loss. Lyn's ashes were taken to the main Buddhist Temple Cemetery in Japan to be near the *Dai-Gohonzon*, the ashes of the *True Buddha Nichiren Daishonin, Nichiren Shoshu Buddhist Priests* and lay members. I feel relieved and gratified. It was the first time in both our lives that I could guide Lyn's being to a peaceful and protective place where she would be safe. Through *Nichiren Shoshu Buddhism*, I learned that the energy of the deceased remains in the universe, although the physical body no longer exists. I chant every day for her to arrive at the very next existence with beautiful health karma and life karma.

One day, almost a year after Lyn's death, I saw a scene on television depicting a daughter coming to her mother for forgiveness. The two of them were hugging. It made me realize that I stopped hugging Lyn when she became a teenager with problems. I became the arbitrator between her and her emotionally cruel father. When her health became compromised and I was the only caretaker for thirty years, I froze some of my emotions. This enabled me to survive and fulfill Lyn's needs. Amid this, I was a teacher with responsibilities, completing my Master's Degree and dealing with personal issues. Four years into Lyn's continually stressful marriage, I stepped back from caring for her physical situation to some degree. I began to realize that I was afraid to hug her. Death was hovering over Lyn. I didn't know how I could deal with the pain of losing her. I was trying to protect myself from the trauma. I made the decision to give her the hugs she needed every time we greeted and parted from one another. A week before her death, we spent about four hours together. I hugged her when we greeted. When we were ready to say goodbye, I felt sudden fear inside of me. I fell back from where she stood onto the opposite wall for support. I was afraid to hug her!

Lyn knew that she could tell me anything about her thoughts, her relationships and her life in general. It would be safe with me. In our daily conversations, there was a mutual "I love you" when we said good-bye. We can't say that often enough to those we care about. They could cease to exist at any time.

Reliving the deceased's painful experiences, repeatedly, makes closure more difficult. I recall the protective and loving closeness with my daughter when she was a child. We shared anger, confidences and funny experiences when she was a young adult. In her late teens and early twenties, Lyn was physically beautiful, socially vibrant and she loved to dance. Lyn adored horses, enjoyed riding them and showed a huge Arabian mare for the actor Burgess Meredith. As Lyn matured, there were mutual loving confidences, happy times, disturbing ones and the stress of medical emergencies. They are all reminders of her existence within my life for sixty years. During my daily activities, I relive incidents of our emotional togetherness. I remember her compassion, her unlimited love, the factual knowledge she collected and shared to help people. Despite her illnesses, Lyn completed her Master's Degree in Psychology. She worked with young adults who had neurological and/or emotional problems. She was the "mother" of all of them. They and her pets were the children she never could have because of early diabetic problems. Verifying her life as it was joined to mine is an emotional and heartfelt reminder of the love we shared that will always be "here" with me.

When Lyn passed, I was a *Nichiren Shoshu Buddhist*, and had already experienced the *Journey to Now*. The protocol enabled me to clarify my life in the NOW, without the encumbrance of old trauma reactions. Chanting *Nam-Myoho-Renge-Kyo* purifies my focus and vision of reality. It helps me understand how karmic energies have a bearing on my daily life choices. I used this protocol to constructively cope with my grieving and it supported my efforts to make my life as gratifying as possible. That honors myself and my daughter Lyn Carrie Smith.

Фот. В. Нѣмцовъ.

My mother Sonetta (Sophie) was photographed in Russia. Her mother died when she was twelve. She and her younger brother were raised by a stern but fair father.

CHAPTER 20

You Can Understand Addiction

"We crave toxic substances we have an excess of," (sugar, salt, caffeine, nicotine, street or medical drugs) was the wisdom Dr. Max Warmbrand N. D., D. O., D. C. shared with me in 1956.

He emphasized the interaction of body and mind energies. Dr. Warmbrand said that all organs and glands are affected by ingested substances. They move through the bloodstream and the nervous system, influencing our emotions and brain functioning. Over time, Dr. Warmbrand would remind me of how our emotional/physical functioning interconnects. He spoke about emotional distress that changes the chemical balance of the physical body and physical problems that effect emotional balance. Dr. Warmbrand said that it is hard to determine whether an illness originated from emotional stress or physical problems. The comprehensive information Dr. Warmbrand freely shared was the stimuli for the concept of *Understanding Addiction*.

I discovered the term homeostasis when I began my collegiate studies in 1960. The dictionary defined it as a tendency towards a state of equilibrium between two different but interdependent elements. An infected toe involves the entire foot's healing process. An effective remedy can stimulate the entire foot's healing process to cure the "sick" toe. The toe and foot become whole in a state of restored health. I connected the dictionary's definition of homeostasis with Dr. Warmbrand's wisdom and from my personal experience with alternative healing. This became the basis for visualizing the development of an *Understanding Addiction* protocol.

In Hans Selye M. D.'s book *The Stress of Life* he writes about the great

French physiologist Claude Bernarad who taught that a most characteristic feature of all living beings is an ability to maintain internal consistency. Dr. Selye states that homeostasis is the organic stability that maintains steadiness in every respect. I realized Dr. Warmbrand's lifestyle protocol that created a balance between one or more elements was homeostasis.

I observed clients who became accustomed to certain levels of food, drugs and emotions that controlled their cognitive and physical functioning. Their behaviors were detrimental to their lives. The lessening of any accustomed effect of an ingested substance or emotion initiates a craving to return to that level we have become accustomed to. There is a constant emotional/physical interaction of factors that always seeks equilibrium.

Intense craving for a specific food or drug does not mean that you need it. You might assume that you are compelled to let that feeling control your actions. You are not weak, stupid or a glutton. Your behavior is a reaction to your body's chemical imbalance. Changes with your diet, changes with drug reliance, exercise, relaxation techniques to correct your body's disharmony will result in the ability to control your behavior.

Dr. Gary Null's *The Food–Mood–Body Connection* states, "The medical community as well as the homeopathic world, now understands that addictions may be diseases, degenerate ones at that." Dr. Null continues, "...To eliminate those addictive pressures that send us into sex addiction, drug addiction, alcohol addiction, violence addiction and overeating. We must get our endorphins and neurotransmitters back to normal levels." Dr. Null refers to Dr. Hodes' four or five-day diversified food rotation diets with a variety of foods and no one food more than twice a week. Dr. Null adds, "Today, there are large numbers of very good alcoholism treatment programs in the United States, where they depend primarily on a combination of a type of nutrition...and...supplements."

Any one thing that you do to yourself, or is done to you, influences every part of your being. We can free ourselves of imposed constraints that effect our lives. It is possible to eliminate these elements we ingest that interfere with the management of our emotional/physical behavior.

Eliminating their influence frees us to become the master of our activity. This enables us to choose more satisfying ways of functioning. No longer must we react to uncomfortable, dominating stimuli. We can rejoice, owning our responsibility for the freedom of choice that can bring emotional behavior and/or physical wellness.

I was introduced to Dr. Warmbrand while in a very stressful marriage. My sinus condition was close to becoming asthmatic. The pain from colitis was so bad I would roll on the floor in a fetal position. My personal experience with Dr. Warmbrand involved the cleansing of toxins from my body and rebuilding it to a healthful state with a beneficial chemical balance from acidic to alkaline. It improved my health and eliminated pain. I changed my diet and the foods I began to desire correlated with what I was eating more of. That included raw vegetable salads, fruits, nuts, seeds, whole grains, fish, tofu with vitamins and herbs. In time, my diet became vegan.

Prior to changing my diet, a certain level of sugar I was accustomed to, altered my ability to function. I became tired and was less efficient mentally and psychically. Using less sugar than I was accustomed to enabled me to overcome my craving for it. I sought an equilibrium that involved my emotional and physical efforts to cleanse and rebuild health. An improved lifestyle created a more healthful chemical balance. I no longer felt the pain from colitis and my nervous system was more relaxed. I felt physically and emotionally stronger and was more capable of coping with that troubled marriage. I found constructive ways to guide that pressured relationship, making it bearable enough until I could leave. My path towards getting out, meant adding the intellectual strain of beginning college at thirty years of age, while I was coping with marital strife and trying to protect my children from tension. The goal was to earn my degree, begin teaching in the public-school system, establish my financial independence and make it possible for me and my two children to leave this emotionally abusive relationship. Two years after I began teaching, that was exactly what I did.

Free

Free from all those things
Imprisonment brings.
From emotions imposed
From the drugs I chose.
I've opened myself bare
Because I do care
To begin learning
All I've been yearning.
I can start knowing
I can start growing
Learning to love me
To live my life free,
Free from all those things
Imprisonment brings.

At our very first meeting, Dr. Warmbrand told me, "This is the first day of a new life for you" and wrote "prescriptions" to guide my journey. I treasure them and have included them at the end of this chapter.

Dr. Warmbrand suggested I get a degree involving health so he could train me to become his assistant. I investigated subject requirements, including organic and inorganic chemistry. I knew that I couldn't master those subjects. I was always interested in psychology and why people acted as they did. I concentrated on a Counseling M. E. degree. In 1974, I became a *Nichiren Shoshu Buddhist.* Chanting and Buddhist studies helped me realize that it was karma that influenced repetitive behavior. We could only change our own karma, not anyone else's. That influenced the development of *Life Motivating Counseling* in 1983. Clients briefly noted their emotions and reactions on charts daily. I suggested simple answers such as feelings of love, anger, fear, happiness, sadness or apathy to help the client focus on basic issues. These notations were discussed at our weekly sessions. *Daily Social Behavior, Successful Procedures for Goal Change* and *Building Sound Relationships (Observations Prior to Commitment)* are charts that are included at the end of this chapter. The results of our weekly observations focused on what was usually one consistent underlying behavior problem. It was primarily anger or fear that had an impact on varied areas of their social functioning. The goal was to have clients guide their adjustments for daily social interactions and function in a less stressful and a more personally gratifying interactive mode.

The *Life Motivating Counseling* charts became the basic premise for courses I taught at Rockland Community College located in Suffern, New York. *Successful Procedures for Goal Change*, and *Building Sound Relationships* drew a grateful response. It moved me deeply. After class one student cried. She told me she wished that someone had offered this information to her before she chose a husband she had to divorce. She was now responsible with caring for two children as a single parent.

Generations of parents and grandparents' social interactions that are like those of the client, is referred to as karmic in *Nichiren Shoshu Buddhism* and as family neuroses in psychology. Behavior that is a "repetitive energy functioning pattern" can include reenacting the initial trauma reaction when specific environmental stimuli effects it. A definition of karma from the *Collected Sermons of High Priest Nikken Shonin (1992-2002)* is, "Internal causes residing in the depths of life that manifest themselves as conspicuous effects when external causes or conditions are encountered. All people possess both positive and negative karma." (For validated *Nichiren Shoshu Buddhist* clarifications, go to www.nst.org). My observations of the recurrent emotional/physical reactions from clients' primary childhood trauma led to the development of the *Journey to Now*.

Changes in diet, exercise, chanting *Nam-Myoho-Renge-Kyo* and utilizing the *Journey to Now Protocol* enabled me to further clarify my focus on beneficial pursuits. This energy extended to my family, friends, clients and the world around me. It reaffirmed Dr. Warmbrand's observation of the constant emotional/physical interactive process that starts within us and affects the environment surrounding us.

The first time I became aware of alternative health information was in 1949, when I discovered Dr. Carlton Fredericks' radio program. Dr. Fredericks was informative and offered his own vitamin formulas. He maintained a residence in Rockland County. It was with his help that I and others prevented fluoride from being introduced into the Rockland County water system.

It was inspiring to learn how some people matured into the kind of healers they became. In 1960, I met Dr. Alice Chase, an osteopathic physician who lived in Rockland County, New York. I respected her determination to follow her ideals as a suffragist. She won the battle that prevented her from being admitted to medical school because she was a woman. She became a surgeon to understand how to help clients avoid the need for surgery. It was Dr. J.H. Tilden's book *"Toxin Theory,"* that influenced Dr. Chase's decision to convert her medical practice to alternative health. She freely shared her practical approach to alternative medicine with me and her other clients. Her supportive attitude in times of need was gratifying. Dr. Chase attended my graduation when I earned my B. E. from St. Thomas Aquinas College in 1968. She was proud of my efforts.

In 1956, Dr. Warmbrand told me that he was born in Austria and had tuberculosis of the joints when he was young. The doctors cut out his hip bone, leaving him with a severe limp and told him he was going to die. Dr. Warmbrand was determined to live. He read a doctor's book that taught him how to cleanse (detoxify) and rebuild his body to a healthful state. He came to the United States, enrolled in the University of Texas and earned his naturopathic degree at the same time Dr. Gaylord Hauser did. How fortunate it was that special books influenced both Dr. Warmbrand and Dr. Chase who became healers and helped so many of us make our lives better.

Dr. Warmbrand passed on at around the age of eighty-five. This created a void in my life. I missed the love he gave so freely. I was at a loss to seek alternative health care guidance for me, my family and friends. In the 1970s, I became aware of the Steiner Foundation in Rockland County, where Dr. Gerald Karnow and Dr. Paul Scharff offered homeopathic guidance. In 1982, I began listening to Dr. Gary Null's radio program on WBAI/FM and in 2006 to his Progressive Radio Network (www.prn.fm). The health information he and other experts offered was valuable for myself and for those I shared it with. Dr. Null, with his courageous persona, spoke the truth publicly about health care issues and world issues. He offered guidance to practitioners who were being attacked because they were not practicing allopathic medicine. Until that time, alternative health care professionals were generally careful to avoid public recognition for fear of persecution. These doctors now felt safe enough to practice openly. They expressed their views on radio, television, with books, DVDs and lecturing. I have personally shared Dr. Gary Null's books, cassettes, videos and DVDs to many others who needed and desired this information.

Despite his busy schedule, Dr. Gary Null always seems to find time to answer anyone's health related questions and he has helped me survive since 1982. Watching how he functioned helped me understand how I could concentrate on my own wellbeing, help others and pursue the career I love. It is a heartwarming experience to observe clients, who have learned to help themselves with the *Journey to Now Protocol*.

Since 1956, I was fortunate to know professional caretakers who have offered knowledge that I in turn, could pass on to others. They showed compassion for those in need, helping clients without available finances, studying to do the best for clients, listening to clients' needs and including them in the healing process. Max Warmbrand, N. D., D. O., D. C., Marshal Kaufer, D. O., Alice Chase, D. O., Sandra Dietch, Midwife, Dr. Gerald Karnow, Dr. Paul Scharff, William H. Philpott, M. D., Patrick A. Grisafi, M. D., Michael Schachter, M. D., Naomi Pelzig, M. D., Steven Glassman, Advanced Certified Rolfer, Dr. Barbara Cohen, Gary Null, PhD, Howard Robins, D. P. M., Martin Feldman, M. D., Howard Hinden, D. D. S., Joseph Hazucha, C. S. W., Ron Wish, M. D., David Johnston, D. O., Dorothy Whitten, M.S., R. N., H. N., C. H. T., Luanne Pennisi, R. N., M. S., Daniel Umberger, D. O. and John Juhl D. O. have all helped to prolong my life. I shared my benefits from alternative health care and have introduced and encouraged many to utilize various methods to improve their emotional and/or physical state of being.

I met Dr. Martin Feldman in 1983. He was an allopathic physician and became interested in what Dr Gary Null did. He took the time to observe Dr. Null and studied to become an alternative physician. It was easy to feel affection for this kind, caring, intelligent man. He was a proficient, knowledgeable and concerned doctor. His caring for my whole being cannot be replaced. Dr. Feldman died on January 6, 2015. I felt as though I lost a member of my family.

Dr. Feldman lowered or omitted his fees when patients were unable to pay. He and Dr. Warmbrand, had that same true concern for their patients that took precedent over financial concerns. At a time when finances were problematic, Dr. Warmbrand charged me $10.00 for a full hour visit. Dr. Alice Chase took your financial situation into consideration when determining a fee or didn't ask for one. Presenting a problem to Dr. Gary Null at a casual meeting can result in him freely giving you a full protocol within a minute. He counsels terminal patients without financial compensation. I am honored to have known these and other humane and competent alternative medical practitioners.

Universe Energies

Truth is our own external environment
Reflects internal energies we vent
Creating an effect within and without
Universe energies, also about
The sun's atmosphere that's so far away
Affecting each one every night and day,
To function internally, external
Is what we have been taught by one and all.
These false boundaries make us feel so safe,
Me, you, them, it, separations we make
So why does our joy reflect on others

Our misery weighs heavy on brothers.
Energy containment does not exist
Limitless boundaries cannot be fixed.
Me, you, them, it and universe energies
A oneness that flows through you and me.

The *Journey to Now Protocol* can help you recognize the way your emotional and physical responses affect each other. These observations can prevent reliving your old trauma reactions again and again. *Understanding Addiction* is an adjunct to the protocol. It provides guidance to reassess your functioning with an encouraging process for avoiding drugs such as heroin. These drugs offer relief from aggravated emotions of fear, anxiety, etc., but when the extreme euphoria of a dose wears off, the stress that reappears seems more intense and insurmountable than before. That creates a desperation for an immediate dose to alleviate that unbearable experience. It is a torturous cycle to maintain.

Problems

Most people have problems
Some have them because of
Themselves, some because of
Others and some...because.

Albert Einstein said that we should learn from yesterday, live for today and hope for tomorrow. We can change that word HOPE to the word WORK, for tomorrow's improved life conditions, for ourselves, those in our personal environment and for the world. In the *Nichiren Shoshu Buddhist* practice, the *Shinjikan Sutra* states, "If you want to understand the causes that existed in the past, look at the results as they are manifested in the present. And if you want to understand what results will be manifested in the future, look at the causes that exists in the present."

Understanding Physical Addiction

1. Sit comfortably, closing your eyes and take in a deep breath, through your nose, with your stomach expanding. Hold that breath a bit. Let more of the breath out through your mouth than you breathed in through your nose. Do that with your stomach receding. Repeat until you feel relaxed. Continue throughout this protocol as much as is possible.

2. Picture a "justice scale."

3. Hold both hands high at the same level to signify scales.

4. We will use the word "heroin" to represent cravings.

5. The right side of the scale denotes a 100% level of heroin in the body. The left side of the scale held at the same level denotes maintaining a 100% level of heroin in the body.

6. The body feels comfortable with its ACCUSTOMED 100% level of heroin.

7. When the left hand is lowered it denotes a 50% loss of heroin in the body.

8. How does the body react to less than the 100% level of heroin it is ACCUSTOMED to?

9. With a 50% lessening of the ACCUSTOMED 100% level of heroin in the body chemistry, the discomforts of physical and emotional pain are unbearable.

10. Desperation causes one to do anything to rid the body of those aches and pains. It craves the heroin that can bring the body back to its ACCUSTOMED 100% level of heroin.

11. Lifting the left arm to the same level as the right arm signifies the restoration of the ACCUSTOMED 100% level of heroin in the body needed to regain physical and emotional comfort.

12. This general process holds true for drugs, salt, sugar, nicotine, alcohol, etc.

13. The key premise of craving is based on what the body becomes ACCUSTOMED to.

14. The ACCUSTOMED level of heroin (salt, sugar, nicotine, drugs, alcohol, etc.) can be reversed by gradually lowering the ACCUSTOMED intake level of those addictive elements.

15. Cravings can be diverted by altering the body's chemical balance. A good approach is to develop a diet rich in organic fruits, vegetables, whole grains, tofu, nuts and fish. Manageable desires for healthful food intake will correlate with the body's chemical balance as it improves. We can become ACCUSTOMED to being in control of our chosen beneficial cravings. Professionally monitored protocols are available as they are needed.

Brain Allergies, the Psycho Nutrient Connection by William H. Philpott, M.D., and Dwight K. Kalita, PhD notes the considerable progress that has been made in connecting the relationship between the physical and the addictive. It refers to Robert O. Becker's research verifying that negative electromagnetic energy does heal.

In the magazine, *Magnetic Health Quarterly* established in 2000 by William H. Philpott, M.D., in the chapter *Addiction*, he writes that with addictions such as cocaine, morphine, nicotine, tobacco, etc., the subject feels euphoric and judgment is impaired. Three or four hours later, a withdrawal phase sets in, with the drop in the narcotic substance due to acidity and lack of oxygen. Withdrawal symptoms are usually relieved within ten minutes with the use of magnets. Included in this protocol is a four-day diversified rotation diet with frequently used foods to be eaten once every fourth day.

The National Acupuncture Detoxification Association (NADA) conducts education and training related to the use of specific ear acupuncture. The NADA protocol offers comprehensive addiction treatment programs to relieve suffering during detoxification, to prevent relapse and to support recovery. This includes support groups and general health care. The Lincoln Clinic opened in 1974 in the South Bronx borough of New York. It was a pioneer in the use of the NADA protocols. The acupuncture treatments proved so successful that methadone was dropped from the program. In addition to reducing withdrawal symptoms, acupuncture provides a strong, calming effect on substance abuse and substantially reduces drug craving. Clients described feeling relaxed but alert. This affected the patient's state of mind during withdrawal.

Understanding Emotional Abuse includes a varied combination of emotional, physical and sexual abuse. It illustrates how we might accept or reject an accustomed level of

Understanding Emotional Abuse.

1. Sit comfortably, closing your eyes and take a deep breath through your nose with your stomach expanding. Hold that breath a bit. Let out more breath, through your mouth, than you breathed in through your nose. Do that with your stomach reseeding. Repeat until you feel relaxed and continue, as much as possible, throughout this exercise.

2. Picture a justice scale.

3. Hold both hands high at the same level to denote scales.

4. The right hand held high, signifies a 100% level of varying combinations of emotional, physical and sexual abuse.

5. The left hand held high at the same level signifies the maintenance of a 100% level of abuse.

6. The emotional/physical being is ACCUSTOMED to 100% of abuse.

7. The left hand is lowered to denote the loss of a 50% level of abuse.

8. The resultant emotional/physical reaction is confused, anguished and fearful.

9. One does not know how to react without the abuse that one has become ACCUSTOMED to.

10. One may seek other abusive relationships or situations that can reinstate the ACCUSTOMED 100% level of abuse.

11. Without an external abusive environment, one can bring back that ACCUSTOMED 100% level of distress by ingesting drugs, or self-inflicted physical harm.

12. Lifting the left arm to the same level as the right arm signifies a return to the ACCUSTOMED 100% level of abuse. It is familiar to us, so we know how to deal with that fear, anxiety and anguish.

13. Gradually lessening painful, anxious, stressful social interactions and/or self-abuse can help one become ACCUSTOMED to new levels of freedom from that anguish. The *Journey to Now Protocol* experience and other supportive therapies offer alternatives.

14. Those ACCUSTOMED anxieties can be transformed into ACCUSTOMED desires for relationships and situations which are safe, beneficial and pleasing.

Understanding Addiction can make you more aware of how you have maintained emotional and physical stresses in your life. When used in conjunction with *Journey to Now*, it can enhance the way you function and become more joyful.

You can begin to live this adventure with a new freedom.

DAILY SOCIAL BEHAVIOR

Name _____ DATE: From_____ To_____

Monday Tuesday Wednesday Thursday Friday Saturday Sunday

HOW do I feel?

WHY I feel that way?

WHAT doesn't feel right?

What WOULD feel right?

Positive action that CAN make it right?

Action TAKEN to make it right!

Are results SATISFACTORY?

What MORE can I do?

Successful Procedures for Goal Change   Name: _____

Date: _____

           Monday Tuesday Wednesday Thursday Friday Saturday Sunday

Desired Goal Change

Fears for Change

Childhood Similarities

Avoidance Techniques for Change

Research: Change Preparation

Capacity

Realization

Fearless Advance

Successful? Why?

Not Successful?

Why?

Preparation for New Goal

Building Sound Relationships – Observation Prior to Commitment

Name: _____   Date: _____

	Monday	Tuesday	Wednesday	Thursday	Friday	Saturday	Sunday
Preferred Recreation							
Preferred Foods							
Clothing Preferences							
Potential Home Location							
Career Goals							
Financial Goals							
Social Interactions							
Children? How Many?							
Successful Compromise							
Negotiations?							
Adjust Relationship?							
Y/N Why?							

Dr. Max Warmbrand's Prescription

At our very first meeting, Dr. Warmbrand
told me I was beginning a whole new life.

FIRESIDE 8-1969   REG. No. 72

DR. MAX WARMBRAND
NATUREOPATHIC PHYSICIAN

1747 SUMMER STREET   STAMFORD, CONN.

NAME_____ AGE_____

ADDRESS_____ DATE_____

R̠   *Breakfast*

1.) *Fresh fruit — one kind of fruit at a time*

2.) *Very ripe banana (if still hungry)*

This is the first prescription (of seven) Dr. Warmbrand wrote for me at my very first visit with him in 1959.

FIRESIDE 8-1969   REG. No. 72

DR. MAX WARMBRAND
NATUREOPATHIC PHYSICIAN

1747 SUMMER STREET   STAMFORD, CONN.

NAME_____AGE_____

ADDRESS_____DATE_____

℞

Noon :—

1.) Raw Vegetable Salad

2.) 1-2 steamed vegetables
(no salt, no butter)

3.) Stewed prunes or stewed
peaches or any stewed
fruit or berries for
dessert (no sugar
no crea—

FIRESIDE 8-1969   REG. No. 72

DR. MAX WARMBRAND
NATUREOPATHIC PHYSICIAN

1747 SUMMER STREET   STAMFORD, CONN.

NAME_____AGE_____

ADDRESS_____DATE_____

℞ *Eve :*

1.) Raw Vegetable Salad

2.) Small portion of chicken
    or lean fish or any lean
    meat every 2nd day

on alternate days:
        Baked Potatoes.

3.) 1-2 Steamed Vegetables
4.) Stewed fruit or blueberries
                    for dessert.

181

FIRESIDE 8-1969   REG. NO. 72

DR. MAX WARMBRAND
NATUREOPATHIC PHYSICIAN

1747 SUMMER STREET   STAMFORD, CONN.

NAME_____ *IV*_____AGE_____

ADDRESS_____DATE_____

R₂

Eat slowly

Chew your food well

Don't eat unless hungry

Don't overeat

FIRESIDE 8-1969   REG. NO. 72

DR. MAX WARMBRAND
NATUREOPATHIC PHYSICIAN

1747 SUMMER STREET   STAMFORD, CONN.

NAME_____ AGE_____

ADDRESS_____ DATE_____

℞

Regular habits after
meal time

Hot bath with 2 glasses
of epsom salt
before retiring

Retire immediately after

FIRESIDE 8-1969 REG. No. 72

DR. MAX WARMBRAND
NATUREOPATHIC PHYSICIAN

1747 SUMMER STREET STAMFORD, CONN.

NAME _____ VI _____ AGE _____

ADDRESS _____ DATE _____

R

Plenty of sleep & rest

Nap or rest period after lunch

No excitement! No tension!

Do everything slowly

Keep your feet warm

NAME

ADDRESS_____DATE

℞ Exercises morning + night

Deep breathing
    ✓X each nostril
    ✓X both nostrils

Leg exercises
    3X each leg
    3X both legs.

CHAPTER 21

Your Journey to Now Protocol

"Marta" was a client who attended school in another country where teachers enforced strict discipline. Children were punished for not reporting a classmate's wrongdoing. This student was obedient and told her teacher that a boy took her pencil. The boy was disciplined. He found her after school when she was alone and punched her in the stomach. Marta was shocked, frightened, physically pained and she felt guilty. From that time into adulthood she suffered severe stomach pains when confronted with the prospect of being hurt emotionally, physically, or financially. This client experienced the *Journey to Now* and it enabled her to live her life in the NOW. Marta still has a very mild sensation when faced with danger. This awareness is a welcome protection from perilous possibilities she can choose to avoid.

I developed *Life Motivating Counseling* with guides to enable the client to record consistently unpleasant daily incidents involving anger, fear and stress. This informational chart was the basis to readily comprehend ongoing social interactions that were disagreeable for adapting desirable behavior. Discussions at weekly sessions resulted in guides for conduct the client felt comfortable with. That positive socialization did not last for long periods, because the basic underlying cause was not recognized and altered. The question was how these stressed emotional/ physical energies originate and what bearing do they have on the present. How can we focus on that initial reaction and utilize it for ongoing behavioral adjustments? The answer was the creation of the *Journey to Now Protocol*. This is your personal guide for satisfactory social behavior.

A key for improving our complicated social behavior is discovering who we really are and how to express that without conflict. This process involves readjusting levels of emotional and physical functioning, by altering the accustomed patterns that are created by childhood traumas.

Feeling conflict is a signal that we do not want to do something we feel obligated to do and don't feel comfortable with. One recycled trauma reaction can create a complex web of discordant and stressful social behavior. This protocol offers you an opportunity to recognize the original emotional pain that created an immediate physical reaction. It helps clarify the current sensation and enables you to decide an action that is beneficial for you. That body sensation may be used to alleviate the conflicted social behavior.

It may seem easier to continue functioning with ongoing emotional and physical stresses that are familiar, rather than risk facing the original trauma. We try to protect ourselves by recycling trauma behavior, recreating old fears, anxieties and anger to avoid change. In that way, we are trying to avoid unfamiliar but anticipated punishment for unpleasant social interactions. We make excuses, tell lies, use verbally and/or physically aggressive behavior to confuse and distract perceived opponents. These defensive mechanisms magnify the stress from continual anxieties and fears. Anticipating what someone's behavior would be, in a caring situation we are not used to coping with, can be frightening. It feels easier to recycle old trauma reactions and relive the abuse we are accustomed to. This fear creates a formidable block to achieving transformation and the adjusting of what seems to be impossible.

We continue to relive the hurtful energies of a childhood trauma even though they are no longer a threat NOW. We perceive current social interactions that have only similar aspects of the original painful experience to be a repetition of that old incident. It is just the trauma reaction that is recycled. Someone could confront us and speak loudly in an aggressive manner as might have occurred in childhood. This is not the original threat, but it still triggers the same danger. In the article *"EFT: Healing for Emotional Trauma, Stress and Anxiety,"* Dr. Lynne Zimmerman, a specialist in energy medicine, writes about the limbic system in the brain. It processes our emotions and it can affect any organ, muscle or system in the body. The original emotional trauma is maintained and recorded in the body and the brain. The experience of something remembered from an earlier trauma produces the same emotions that were felt initially. With the *Journey to Now* we learn to utilize emotional/ physical reactions. It helps us to focus our awareness on hurt or stressed feelings as they occur in a current social situation. We use those responses to remedy the incidents. We can develop a clarified awareness from experiencing this protocol. We begin to function within the reality of NOW and not in our old, habitual and agonizing zone. The journey to NOW process can eliminate recycling our childhood trauma reactions.

The *Journey to Now* is a step by step method. It was created to discontinue patterns of reliving old emotional pain, fear and stress. The utilization of this protocol can help us recognize and focus reactions towards the original painful trauma that we recycle in the HERE and NOW. This is not the actual old danger that is recurring in the present, but our recycling of that reaction. The following protocol clarifies the process by which we have relived past disturbances. Experiencing the completed protocol can help you throw off the shackles of those childhood wounds in the NOW. It establishes how those original reactions can protect you from old pain, fear and stress.

The *Journey to Now Protocol's* breathing technique assists in freeing our recollection of both old and immediate stressful reactions as they occur. In *The Relaxation Response*, Dr. Herbert Benson writes that this process can focus the mind and affect the heart and breathing rate. The realization of how the initial trauma originated and affected us physically may be momentarily disturbing, but the breathing encourages open recognition. It connects that original incident to distressful repetitive social behavior and its effects on social situations in the present. You can learn to utilize those physical sensations from childhood abuse to alert, protect and release yourself from distressful social interactions in the

NOW. You will begin to comprehend the *Journey to Now's* guide in the gradual process of experiencing it.

Sessions should be attempted when you are alone and feeling safe in the environment you choose. For a successful participation, it is vital to make a permanent recording of the protocol sessions verbally and/or visually.

You may complete some of these steps at one sitting and continue the rest at another time. Before you begin again, review the recording of your previous sessions to keep track of your progress.

If you feel uncomfortable at any step, you can stop and evaluate a previous one or go back to Step 1. Beginning again can help to relieve any tension you may be experiencing.

It is only your individuality that determines how you respond to each direction and what your time frame is.

The thirty-six steps are in a specific order. Each one creates a basis for the next one. They support your efforts for attaining a favorable result. Skipping a direction undermines the ultimate purpose of discovering how you can avoid reliving old trauma reactions.

Sit comfortably with hands relaxed.

1. Close your eyes as much as possible through the entire process.

2. Breathe in deeply through your nose, with ONLY your stomach extended as you breathe in.

3. Hold your breath for a moment.

4. Exhale more through the mouth, more than you breathed in, with ONLY the stomach receding as you breathe out.

5. Repeat until you feel relaxed.

6. Maintain closed eyes and continue the deep breathing throughout the entire session, as much as possible.

7. Relax and take your time to respond to these directions in the order in which they are presented. Answers are totally individual and there may be more than one answer. You may wish to review a step before responding.

8. What prominent sensations do you feel in your body at this moment?

9. Is it your stomach, chest, neck, shoulder, etc.?

10. Describe the immediate kind of sensation you are experiencing. It may be pain, aching, throbbing, exciting, joyous, etc.

11. What is your first memory of that feeling?

12. Who and what were involved and when?

13. Describe the hurt, aching, suffering, distress, pain, anger, joy, etc. of that encounter.

14. You can cry, yell, laugh or talk at persons or situations that were involved or still are.

15. Express those feelings as you need to. Your courage to talk, cry, yell, laugh about it helps to overcome being controlled by an old trauma. This helps to free you from being dominated by the past.

16. Tell how and why those persons or situations hurt you, made you fearful or happy.

17. Explain the details of that first trauma. Describe the pain and/or anguish or joy.

18. It can be hurting or happy in the moment, but expressing it, can help release the power it has had over you.

19. It is important to review the last session before beginning the next one. You can build upon your experience rather than repeat it.

20. Do you experience old emotional/physical sensations in present day socializations, to a loud voice or attitude that are reminiscent of the past?

21. How is that recurrence like your childhood trauma reaction?

22. How do you cope with those emotional/physical reactions NOW?

23. Why do you think you react as you do now?

24. How does that current reaction connect to the original trauma?

25. Do you understand that when you recycle just the childhood trauma REACTIONS you are not reliving the original trauma, but are only recreating the REACTION to it?

26. When someone or something hurt you in the past, did you feel the same kind of sensation as you do NOW when you feel hurt?

27. When someone hurts you in similar ways NOW, do you feel the same sensation that you felt in the past?

28. That emotional/physical pain and/or sensation can become your protector.

29. When you feel that sensation in current situations, recognize it and use it to protect yourself.

30. It tells you that you are being hurt.

31. Try to remove yourself from that person or situation quickly as you walk away. For example: "I'd love to stay and talk but I'm

an hour late for an appointment." "Sorry, had to be in 'Frisco an hour ago" or "I have diarrhea and have to run!"

32. If you are able to, you can tell that person "where to go" in a calm, constructive manner, you can do so, only if you think it will help to improve the situation.

33. In time, you may be able to overcome such incidents verbally if you choose not to leave the scene.

34. With practice, you may also learn to clarify and express your relationship standards verbally to affect the immediate situation. When experiencing a person's behavior towards you or to others, it is important that you instantly recognize your immediate emotional/physical reactions. That can help you accept or reject social relationships with your new standards. You may say "Sorry I can't accept that language or behavior, etc." or "Thank you for understanding my needs and responding to them accordingly."

35. Where is your physical reaction when you are told (or tell yourself) that you are courageous, smart, loving, caring? Remember that physical sensation, it tells you when you are safe and can respond to that social situation.

36. Only you can judge how often you want to continue reviewing sessions. They are yours for life.

You may wonder why these same kinds of social situations reoccurred in your life through the years. *Nichiren Shoshu Buddhism* says it is karma; psychology defines it as neurosis. Those concepts are a book in itself. I personally have learned how to change my karma through chanting *Nam-Myoho-Renge-Kyo.* I have altered my social interactions by experiencing *Journey to Now. From Birth to Death with Sex In Between* can help the reader find emancipation from being entrapped by past experiences.

Each time you utilize your *Journey to Now* you are lifting a burden of imposed trauma, creating a distance between the THEN and NOW. You can become more precise when making social decisions. It is the use of this protocol that helps you learn how to instantly recognize and apply emotional/physical sensations. The purpose being to evaluate and effect satisfying social behavior. It is a rewarding asset to apply the protocol's directions. If you find it necessary, refer to therapeutic guidance for clarifying specific issues while using it. It is the journey to NOW that frees the true you to emerge and develop.

CHAPTER 22

Congratulations

Courage is looking fear in the face and searching for constructive ways to conquer it. Congratulations for your courage and determination to enjoy a fulfilling relationship with yourself, others and the world around you. The *Journey to Now* experience helped clients overcome fear, anger and reverse self-destructive lifestyles. They felt freer to express advantageous capacities that had been dormant. For myself, I learned how it was possible to reject those who could hurt me and effect my well-being. I realized my individuality, creativity and intuitive capacities and I enjoy living them.

<u>Sax and Sex</u>

> *The mellow air tones flowing through*
> *Moves breath that falls against my chest*
> *Those sultry hoarse low tones come through*
> *Sensitive fingers on keys rest*
> *Inner lips caress reeds so true*
> *Warm breath whispers love words best*
> *Mellow, enticing sounds play blues.*
> *Skin, breath, music from horn, sex,*
> *The mellow air tones flowing through*
> *Moves breath that falls against my chest.*

I listened to some musicians discuss their awakening to the music they love. There was usually a capacity and attraction for the music at a very young age, as well as encouragement from family and others. The eventual attainment of their world-wide success was due to a continual determined effort, through many years, to take personal responsibility for mastering their instrument. That area of success didn't always correlate with the mastery of personal relationships. This also holds true with those who are accomplished, honored, publicly admired politicians, environmentalists, scientists, artists, musicians, actors and writers.

Experiencing the *Journey to Now* and *Understanding Addiction* offers tools for clarifying who you really are. It enables you to develop a responsibility for less-conflicted behaviors to become prominent in the many-sided aspects of your life. The responsible person becomes one who can determine how to choose and activate productive social interactions. Blaming someone else is a wasted effort.

The word responsibility is interesting. During our childhood, we may have been told it is "responsible" to remember to do chores and finish them. When we didn't do that, the consequences were most likely some punishment. This created the guilt and anger that became associated with the word "responsibility." Being responsible for ourselves gives us the freedom to make favorable decisions and behave only as we would wish to do. It allows us the freedom to misjudge or fail without anyone looking over our shoulders. No one is there to say, "I told you so." We have the freedom to reject our decision, to alter our decision, decide on a new concept and acknowledge the successful efforts of self-evaluations.

The courage to fight against fear offers us the opportunity to explore, create and follow paths of our own choosing. Accepting responsibility for pleasant or unpleasant adventures is an interesting experience. It allows us to become accountable to ourselves. The *Journey to Now* offers the guide for you to become more attuned to the true inner being that effects our social interactions. Focusing on physical signals becomes your guide for safe reactions.

Dr. Gary Null's book *Mind Power* refers to a scientific study showing that those who prayed demonstrated healthier behaviors, better physical functioning and higher mental scores. This could include chanting, meditation and martial arts. *Nichiren Shoshu Buddhism* states that, "A mind which is presently clouded by illusions originating from the innate darkness of life, is like a tarnished mirror. But once it is polished, it will become clear." When we make the effort to attain enlightenment (wisdom, knowledge) and see reality as it exists in the NOW, we can make beneficial decisions that affect our lives.

The practice of the *Journey to Now Protocol* and *Understanding Addiction*, can guide you to develop a working consciousness. This can begin a transition from the ongoing social behavior that had been developed from childhood traumas. It can be more peaceful and truer to our personal needs. The revised consciousness has a bearing on our relationship choices with family, friends, work associations, intimate relationships, interactions with our community and the world we live in. The goal would be for the world to become a more humane society. This can begin with who we become. With compassionate and social compatibility, we can encourage someone, who in turn, transmits that harmonious interaction to another. Caring personal and social rela-tionships, paired with social awareness, active participation in our communities and the world can create the kind of society we would like to live in.

The *Journey to Now* and *Understanding Addiction* guides your under-standing for recycling old traumatic behavior reactions in the HERE and NOW. The ultimate purpose for utilizing old emotional and physical trauma sensations is to protect you from current social distress in the present. The goal is to revise your current social behavior to one that you feel is satisfactory for functioning NOW. *From Birth to Death with Sex In Between* is a travel guide that can prepare you to acknowledge, accept, love and live the total individuality of your life.

Loss and Found

What did I have then that I lost now?
What do I need that I don't get now?
The heart beating and the excitement
From a thrilling time, place, response
That gave me love, sex without effort,
When my oneness would flow and ripple
Nights, days, evenings, mornings were all one
Talking, walking, swimming and loving,
A love supreme in its day and time
And death of that dream I remember.
Time passes with heart, love, growth for now
And my right kind of days, nights, loving
Profound responses as they're needed,
Loyal to the good and bad of me.
What can be more electrifying?

Joy to you!

CHAPTER 23

Afterword

Throughout this book, I focus on the importance of recognizing the physical component of emotional trauma. This can be transformed into an awareness that is spontaneous and self-protective.

Recycling refers to a lifetime of reliving happy or unhappy experiences. "Trauma reactions" describes the emotional and physical components which result from exposure to inflicted pain.

The path *From Birth to Death with Sex In Between* is what you are experiencing. The *Journey to Now Protocol* can free you from repeating painful experiences from the past. This can make it possible to introduce yourself to who you really are and to help focus your energies on the reality of the moment. Cherish that discovery and enjoy living with freedom from those old recycled traumas.

www.ingramcontent.com/pod-product-compliance
Lightning Source LLC
Chambersburg PA
CBHW071951090426
42740CB00011B/1892